3

PEAS IN A

Pram

McKnight
& Bishop
Ltd

ROSIE FARROW

ABOUT THE PUBLISHER

McKnight & Bishop are always on the look-out for new authors and ideas for new books. If you write or if you have an idea for a book, please e-mail: **info@mcknightbishop.com** Some things we love are undiscovered authors, open-source software, Creative Commons, crowd-funding, Amazon/Kindle, social networking, faith, laughter and new ideas.

Visit us at **www.mcknightbishop.com**

All Scripture quotations, unless otherwise indicated, are taken from the Holy Bible, New International Version®, NIV®. Copyright ©1973, 1978, 1984, 2011 by Biblica, Inc.™ Used by permission of Zondervan. All rights reserved worldwide. www.zondervan.com The "NIV" and "New International Version" are trademarks registered in the United States Patent and Trademark Office by Biblica, Inc.™

Scripture quotations from THE MESSAGE. Copyright © by Eugene H. Peterson 1993, 1994, 1995, 1996, 2000, 2001, 2002. Used by permission of NavPress. All rights reserved. Represented by Tyndale House Publishers, Inc.

ISBN 978-1-905691-47-0

A CIP catalogue record for this book is available from the British Library

First published in 2016 by McKnight & Bishop Inspire, an imprint of:
McKnight & Bishop Ltd. | 28 Grifffiths Court, Bowburn, Co. Durham, DH6 5FD
http://www.mcknightbishop.com | info@mcknightbishop.com

This book has been typeset in Garamond-Normal

Printed and bound in Great Britain by Lightning Source Inc, Milton Keynes.
The paper used in this book has been made from wood independently certified as having come from sustainable forests.

"WHERE WERE YOU GOD?"

Where were you God
in the handing over that night?
Where were you God
In the hurt and the pain of rejection?
Where were you God
In the chaos and the madness?
Where were you God
In the darkness and the gloom?
Where were you God
In the loneliness and the heartache?
Where were you God
In the beating and the shame?

I was there.
I visited you,
I comforted you.
I brought light to your darkness.
Now.
Let me bring healing,
Comfort and forgiveness.
I will give you help in this.
I will bring freedom for your
souls.
I sent my son, Jesus, to walk in
your ways.
I sent the Holy Spirit to be your
comforter.
What more could I do?
I am and have done everything!

FAMILY TIMELINE

1929	Leo Harcourt and Audrey Berry married on 31.08.1929.
1930	Birth of Frank on 30.11.1930 to Alice and George Farrow.
1931	Birth of Irene Harcourt 21.09.1931.
1932	St Philomena and the Sacred Heart Church opened on 18.01.1932.
1935	Leo, Audrey and Irene Harcourt sailed to Singapore on 02.03.1935.
1938	This family returned from Singapore on 06.05.1938.
1940	Leo Harcourt travelled to France with the British Expeditionary Force in January 1940. Returned home on 29.05.1940.
1941	Death of Alice Farrow from consumption.
1947	Completion of Cumberland Road Estate.
1948	Frank Farrow started National Service in the Navy for two years.
1949	Irene Harcourt began employment at Peckstons shipping office.
1953	Frank and Ted Farrow sailed to Quebec on 20.05.1953.
1954	Audrey Harcourt died on 09.09.1954 from leukaemia.
1956	Frank and Ted returned to England on 09.02.1956. Frank and Irene met in August 1956. They married on 22.12.1956 in Middlesbrough. Immediately moved to Coventry.
1957	Triplets born on 18.05.1957. Baptised on 20.05.1957. Parents received Queens bounty.
1958	Home address 28 Mary Slessor street, Coventry.
1959	Ann Farrow born on 30.03.1959
1961	7 Windsor road sold. Farrow family did a "moonlight flit" on 13.07.1961. Triplets taken to Nazareth House on 15.07.1961. Parents separated. Grandad Leo and Lily married on 24.07.1961. Ann baptised on 08.09.1961.
1962	Triplets returned to parents on 07.07.1962. Address 5 Mary Ann Street in Middlesbrough.
1965	Triplets took First Holy Communion on 21.01.1965
1967	Farrow family moved to 19 Hereford Close, Cumberland Road Estate, Middlesbrough in October 1967.
1968	Grandad Leo died on 05.02.1968. Triplets enrolled at St Thomas' Senior school in September 1968.
1969	Mary Ann Street demolished along with the Apostolic Church by Compulsory Purchase Order.
1970s	The Greenheld family moved into Hereford Close and a more settled life began.

CHAPTER 1: THE FIRST-BORN

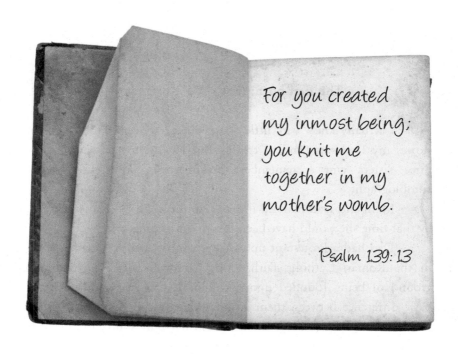

For you created my inmost being; you knit me together in my mother's womb.

Psalm 139: 13

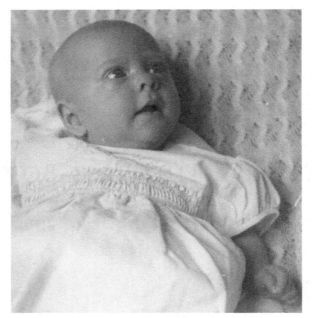

The first-born: that's me, Rosemary.

I actually know very little about our early years, other than the stories my Dad was fond of telling. But I will write down what my three sisters and I remember, making this book a collective autobiography.

Mam and Dad married in haste on the 22nd December 1956, as by that time she would have been four months pregnant.

Dad had a Protestant upbringing whilst Mam's upbringing was in the Roman Catholic faith. Both Churches share the common ground of being founded upon faith in Jesus Christ. However, the basic difference between them is the authority they look to for their beliefs. Protestants embrace the Bible as their only source of authority and faith whilst Roman Catholics view traditions and its Popes to have more than equal authority with the Scriptures.

Therefore, to obtain the priest's permission to marry our parents had to swear an oath to raise their children in the Roman Catholic faith or risk punishment from God.

After the wedding service, which was held at St Mary's RC Church in Linthorpe Village, the couple posed for their photographs outside the church looking very smart in two-piece suits; with no-one realizing that Mam's outfit was a size bigger due to her pregnancy.

 A wedding breakfast was held after the service in The Linthorpe Hotel, but only close family members had an invitation. In love, but apprehensive that people would find out about their secret, Dad travelled back to Coventry, with his new bride, the following day. With Christmas looming, Dad may have had the perfect excuse, with his work in a car manufacturing plant, to make a hasty flight back down South.

It must have been hard for Mam, even at 25 years of age, to leave her childhood home at 7 Windsor Road. She was an only child and was aware that her new husband, Frank, and her father, Leo, didn't get on. Both these men in her life drank a pint or two in the Cleveland Hotel. This pub was situated on Linthorpe Road, just around the corner from Windsor Road. Grandad Leo would watch Dad drinking with his brothers and was appalled by their behavior. Maybe Mam's relationship with Dad would have been nipped in the bud had her mother, Audrey, still been alive.

Sadly she had died from Leukaemia in September 1954 at the age of fifty-one. Her mother would have likely cottoned on to the fact that their daughter was having a baby; but Grandad was oblivious! Five months into her confinement Mam found herself face down on a table in Coventry Hospital. She was surrounded by cushions to make her body more comfortable and an x-ray was taken, so the doctor could determine if she was carrying more than one baby. He soon returned to say, " Mr Farrow, please sit down. You are expecting triplets!"

I have often wondered what strong emotions arose in them both in response to this surprising news. Was it disbelief, followed quickly by dismay at the thought of having so little money? Then worrying about how they would cope with so many mouths to feed. Dad always joked and said he wanted a football team so three little boys would have been a good start. Their names were chosen; Francis, Carl and Michael.

Shortly after this insight into her condition, Mam was taken into Gulson Hospital for bed rest. This enforced stay was to last four months, with iron injections given weekly into her bottom to build up her strength. "I was used like a pin cushion", Mam always stated.

During this period a lovely staff nurse on the ward arranged for baby items and clothing to be donated and collected in preparation for our arrival. Poor Mam had no other help available, as she was no longer in touch with her father or Cecelia (her best friend from their schooldays). Thank Heaven for the kindness of strangers. In addition to this, the National Health Service did not provide for multiple births in the 1950s. Nowadays the Internet has websites providing practical information for parents expecting twins or multiple births.

One such site, twinsuk.co.uk, states it is worth:

a) Contacting the social services department.
b) Contacting the charity, Home Start, who provide trained volunteers to help for a few hours a week.
c) Contacting a company called Baby Em, who provide a Maternity Nurse for a two day or two -week placement.
d) Buying a book titled, "Twins & Multiple Births: The Essential Parenting Guide From Pregnancy to Adulthood" by Dr Carol Cooper. Her book offers first-hand experience and advice.

One mother of triplets is quoted as saying, " The financial side of having triplets is crippling. I spend £50 per week on nappies, wet wipes and milk, not including food and clothing!"

On 18th May 1957 we made our appearance into the world. Mam said it was like shelling peas! Surprise, surprise: three baby girls were born and we were given the names of the nurses who cared for us.

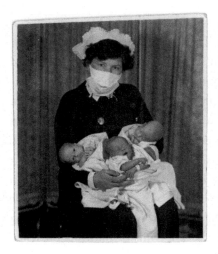

Gulson Hospital, Coventry

Our baptism records show:

- Rosemary born at 8.14 pm, weighed 5lb 9oz
- Frances born at 8.15 pm weighed 4lb 3oz
- Gillian born at 9.06 pm weighed 4lb 3oz

However, a newspaper cutting dated 20th May 1957 states the birth times as 8.40 pm, 8.50 pm and 8.56 pm – Mam and Dad's version?

CERTIFICATE OF BAPTISM

Triplets Born to Coventry Woman

Triplets—all girls—were born to Mrs. Irene Farrow, of 18, Harris Road, Coventry, at Gulson Hospital, Coventry, on Saturday night.

The babies and Mrs. Farrow were to-day said to be doing well.

The first baby, Rosemary, was born at 8.40 p.m. and weighed 5lb. 9oz. Frances was born ten minutes later. She and Gillian, born after another 16mins., each weighed 4lb. 3oz.

It was the first time triplets had been born at the hospital for several years.

Coventry Evening Telegraph, 20th May 1957

After the birth we were quickly taken to the Intensive Care Unit. There must have been some concern that we would not survive, as I hold a certificate of baptism, by a Reverend F. C. Harkin, for two days after our birth and taking place in the hospital. But survive we did!

Back in Middlesbrough, Grandad Leo was to get the surprise of his life! He had sadly lost all contact with his daughter (our mother), Irene, and had not heard from her for months as his letters to her kept returning "address unknown". We had always understood that a neighbour had seen a Midlands newspaper cutting stating "Triplets born to Coventry woman" and promptly knocked on Grandad's door to tell him the news.

However, Uncle Alan remembers a Mr Brannigan being told this news in the pub by someone on Dad's side of the family. Mr Brannigan lived only two doors away from Grandad Leo and was good friends with him. On hearing this information, Mrs Brannigan went straight round to tell Leo, who immediately cycled to Acklam to impart this knowledge to his nephew Alan and wife Cecelia. They, too, had been desperate for any news of Irene and were just as concerned about her as their Uncle. I can only imagine their joint delight as the worry of the previous months fell away to be replaced by this amazing stroke of luck that was to send Grandad Leo on the earliest train to Coventry.

In the 1950s a baby would only be allowed home when its birth weight increased to 6lbs. As I was a very healthy birth weight, I quickly gained the required ounces and was the first of the triplets to leave the hospital. Mam said she practiced on me first; with Frances and Gillian staying in under the nurses' care. On arriving at Gulson Hospital in Coventry as quickly as he was able, Leo found to his dismay, that we had all been discharged! Hospitals had strict rules about giving out private information. Grandad was distraught at this calamity and pleaded with the staff to let him have his daughter's forwarding address. Much to his relief they finally relented, giving him directions to our home.

Now it was Mam's turn to be surprised. Hearing knocking at her front door, she opened it to find her father standing before her. What a reunion that must have been! Grandad would have been brought up-to-date about the fact that the hospital staff had had some difficulty in rearing my two smaller sisters but by the August of 1957 all three of us were in excellent health.

There was no evidence of any abnormality and our weights had increased to 10lb 13½oz, 9lb 14 oz and 9lb 7½oz at three months old. He never went anywhere without his camera and Mam took a photograph of him holding us for the first time.

PLEASE QUOTE THIS NUMBER
IF ANY FURTHER COMMUNICATIONS
E.20621 E.20622 E.20623
BIRMINGHAM REGIONAL HOSPITAL BOARD
No. 20 GROUP. HOSPITAL MANAGEMENT COMMITTEE.

COVENTRY AND WARWICKSHIRE HOSPITAL

Memo from
Dr. H. PARRY WILL

Dear Dr. Wadon,

Date 22nd August, 1957

re Patient Rosemary, Frances & Gilliam Farrow, 3/12
20 Mary Slessor Street, Willenhall.

On the 18.5.57 Mrs. Farrow was delivered of triplets, all girls, weighing 5 lb. 9 oz., 4 lb. 3 oz., and 4 lb. 3 oz.

We had some difficulty in rearing the two smaller babies, but they are now all three in excellent health and there is no evidence of any abnormality. Their weights are 10 lb. 13½ oz., 9 lb. 14¾ oz., and 9 lb. 7½ oz. respectively.

Yours sincerely,

Paediatric Registrar

Dr. Wadon,
83 St. James's Lane.

JAB/KLA

13

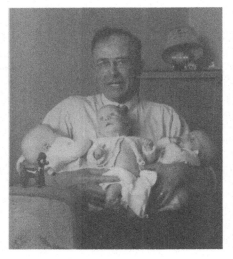

Amongst what little remains of any family records there is an envelope, dated 10th August 1957, showing that Grandad Leo wrote to his mother from Coventry to Portsmouth, suggesting he stayed there long enough to get acquainted with his new granddaughters, writing to let her know what had happened and what he had found.

Grandad Leo returned home to Middlesbrough very excited after being reunited with his family. He had recently retired from the Army and was in employment at Head Wrightson's as an engineer. His workplace was close to the Transporter Bridge and to Leader's, a local wood merchant. He bought some timber there and laden with materials returned home to Linthorpe Village by bus, to begin making highchairs for his three grandchildren.

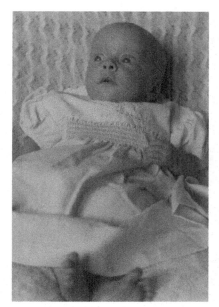 

In December 1957 he caught the train back to Coventry. With his case, Christmas presents and three highchairs strapped to his back he must have looked quite a sight!

Mam would have been so relieved to see the high-chairs coming through the door, as she was struggling to feed three babies propped up in one large armchair. Nowadays it would probably be a health & safety issue, not just for us, but also for Mam's aching back.

CHAPTER 2 – FAMILY

God sets the
lonely in families.

Psalm 68: 6

Dad and Mam were like chalk and cheese in their personalities, upbringing and family life. Dad was born on 30th November 1930 to Alice and George Farrow. He was one of nine children, but sadly two of his brothers died in early infancy.

Grandad George then worked as a labourer at the Rolling Mills for a local iron and steel works in Middlesbrough, most probably Dorman Long & Co. This company became Britain's biggest iron and steel maker employing 33,000 men. Some of these labourers are famous for building what was then the new Tyne Bridge in Newcastle/Gateshead (with the construction beginning in August 1925 and ending in February 1928) and the Sydney Harbour Bridge in Australia! The construction of this larger bridge began in July 1923 with a grand opening taking place on 19th March 1932, with about seventy-nine percent of the steel used being imported from England with the help in some small way of Grandad George.

The family lived in a small cottage at Fairy Dell near Marton, on the Southern edge of Middlesbrough. Alice would have had her hands full caring for their large brood of children!

In 1939, with the threat of World War II looming, many children living in the towns and cities of Great Britain were evacuated from their homes. This action was taken to remove them from the danger of aerial bombing expected on their homes and schools, particularly in Middlesbrough, due to it being an industrial area with docks for shipbuilding, making it vulnerable to bombing. The Farrow family were no exception with the children evacuated to Scarborough. The boys hated this experience so much that they were to find their way home several times. This was a 48-mile journey and they would hide in the hedgerows and eat anything they could lay their hands on. No wonder the authorities eventually decided it was safer for them to remain in the care of their mother!

When Dad was eleven years of age, in 1941, his mother died of consumption, also known as TB (tuberculosis). His father began to spend more of his free time in the public house, no doubt drowning his sorrows at the loss of his wife. The care of the family was eventually taken over by the two eldest daughters, Mary and Katie. The sisters had returned to the family home, now in Pelham Street, in Middlesbrough, after taking pity on the plight of the five wayward boys who were poverty stricken and running amok. As they grew older, the lads loved playing table football as well as football both in and out of school. Then between the ages of eighteen and twenty the five young men completed their National Service which lasted for two years. Some of the lads had taken to smoking, with Dad beginning at 17 years of age.

Eric (his nickname was Greg as he was very friendly with people) served in the Army alongside Colin and Gerry. Ted joined the Air Force and Frank (Dad) served in the Navy. All the lads returned home safely and Grandad George, who himself had served in the First World War, promptly took them all out to the pub for a celebratory drink.

In the following months it came to light that Eric had found himself involved with the Berlin Air Lift and helped clear the infamous Belsen prisoner-of-war camp. He was never to speak about this part of his life even to his wife, Val.

Shortly after leaving the Navy, Dad and his brother Ted set sail on the "Columbia" from Southampton (Gateway to the World) to Quebec. The date was 20th May 1953 and it appears they were soon employed laying electric wires and pipelines in the desolate wastes of Canada. Several stories were told of the adventures had by them both. One involved the brothers freeing brown bears held in cages -which might easily have happened. Dad loved wildlife and would have seen this early example of eco-terrorism as being his civic duty. Another taller tale, perhaps after a bottle or two of Canadian beer, was of a mysterious First Nation squaw who knocked at the door of their cabin asking for a hot drink. When Dad returned with it, she had disappeared without leaving footprints in the snow!

Dad must have lost his passport, as it was renewed on 9th February 1956 in Ottawa and the brothers returned to England on 15th April 1956 with a Finnish friend in tow.

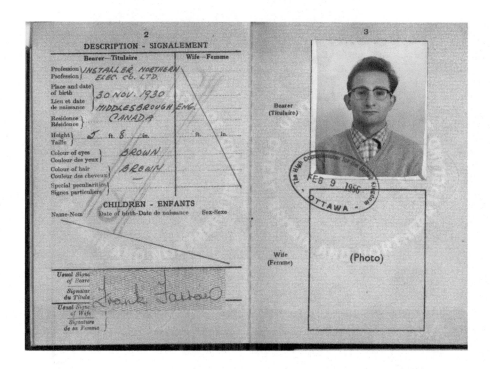

On returning to Middlesbrough, Dad heard there was work to be had in Coventry, then an industrial powerhouse. This city had suffered severe bomb damage during November 1940 in the Second World War in a raid known as the "Coventry Blitz". Historical buildings were in a ruinous state and were demolished to make way for modern developments, altering the infrastructure almost beyond recognition. Coventry's motor industry boomed during the 1950s and 1960s and Dad found employment as a storeman for a local car manufacturer, part of Coventry's "golden age".

Mam was born on 21st September 1931 at the Louise Margaret Hospital in Aldershot. She was the only child of Leo and Audrey Harcourt who christened her Irene Marie.

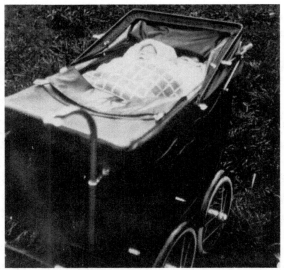

Aldershot is known as the "Home of the British Army". Her father was an Armament Staff Sergeant based in the Guernsey Quarters at the barracks there. His Army career shaped Mam's early years, as on 2nd March 1935 the family set sail for Singapore.

The following three years were lonely for Mam, as it was for all the army children in the far-flung corners of the British Empire. They rarely saw their fathers, whilst their mothers' lives involved entertaining the officers' wives, leaving the young children to be cared for by the local Punjabi native women. How strange and curious this mix of Chinese, Malay, Indian and Western cultures must have seemed after the children's upbringing in England!

Mam was to be over six years old before the family returned to England again. This was on 6th May 1938. Life then became more "normal", as the family settled in Middlesbrough. Joining St Philomena's School, Mam was put in the year below her age group of seven years due to the fact of the limited education she had had abroad. Because of this, she met a girl called Cecelia who was to become her best friend all through her education.

Mam's father, Leo, continued in active service, going overseas with the British Expeditionary Force to France in January 1940. Leo later told my Dad that he evaded capture and took flight clinging to the underside of a lorry. He made his way to Dunkirk in time for the now legendary evacuation on the beaches. An order was given by Winston Churchill for any ship or boat to pick up the stranded men via the harbour and my Grandad Leo happened to be one of the troops to return home safely on 29th May 1940. Thanks to the bravery shown by men and women of the small boat Armada, some 338,226 soldiers were rescued and it was named "the miracle of Dunkirk".

Grandad Leo was not always so fortunate and was injured during his army career. He was being driven through enemy territory and foolishly had his arm resting on the jeep with the window down. The enemy opened fire and hit his hand. I understand this caused a few health problems later in life, but did not prevent his rapid rise through the ranks due to his "exemplary" military conduct, reaching the rank of Captain before the time of his discharge in 1941.

Unlike Dad, however, Mam was dispatched to the countryside to live with an Aunt during the war years and she remembered being taught how to use her gas mask at school. With the horrors of chemical warfare still relatively fresh in the minds of the generation that had survived the first World War, it was drummed into the children, day after day, how important it was that they carried the mask around with them in case of an attack.

Financially secure in her upbringing, Mam attended Sacred Heart School and Church and completed her education at St Mary's

Convent in the centre of Middlesbrough. On leaving the convent at 18 years of age Mam showed little interest in obtaining work, but, encouraged by her mother, found employment as a clerk at Peckston's, the local shipping office. Mam's time there was fun-filled and she formed life-long friendships with her cousin Alan, Cecelia, Val and Eric (Dad's brother). Peckston's sailed Dutch type coasters from the United Kingdom mainly to Finland.

It was at Peckston's that Eric and his future wife, Val, introduced their friend, Irene, to Frank. He had returned home for a two- week holiday because the car manufacturers closed their factories for a two-week period in August each year. Irene and Frank began courting and, as Dad swept Mam off her feet, our parents spoke of plans to emigrate to Canada. But these dreams came to an abrupt halt, as it became clear that Mam was "in the family way". I can imagine her secretly writing to him, informing Dad of this turn of events and insisting they get married as quickly as possible. Having a child out of wedlock was a source of shame and deeply frowned upon in those days. The wedding date was set for 22nd December 1956.

That November Mam visited Cecelia to ask her to be Matron of Honour at her wedding. The two friends went shopping for the wedding outfits. Although Cecelia noticed that Irene chose a suite size larger than normal, she, naively, gave it no further thought. She herself was about six months pregnant after marrying Alan earlier that year. Mam was very slim and, although people began to comment that she had put on a bit of weight, they, too, gave it no further consideration.

Within four months of meeting, our parents were married.

CHAPTER 3 – FLIGHT

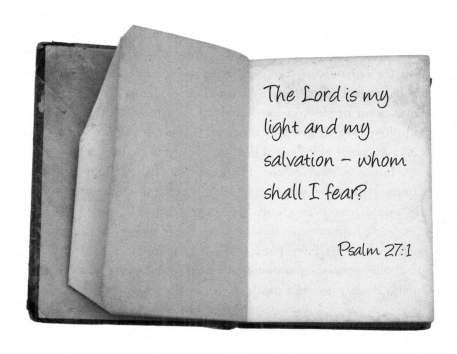

The Lord is my
light and my
salvation – whom
shall I fear?

Psalm 27:1

Now married, our parents were living in Coventry in rented accommodation at 18 Harris Road. The landlady told Mam in no uncertain terms that they would have to find somewhere else to live when the babies were born. At this time Dad had employment as a wirer at the local telephone works.

As Mam lay in Gulson Hospital enduring her enforced stay, it would have been down to Dad to visit the County Borough of Coventry to explain their predicament and that he and his wife would need a new home to bring their three new babies up in! They were allocated a Council house on St James' Estate. Our new address was 28 Mary Slessor Street, part of a Coventry Corporation Housing Development. This was to be our home for the next four years.

Shortly after our birth, Dad was approached to give permission for his three baby daughters to be involved in advertising formula milk. This would have given our parents much-needed additional funds for our ongoing care but he refused. The reason he gave was that he wanted us to have a "normal" upbringing. We never heard Mam's point of view on his decision! One piece of advice that they did follow was a tip given by the family doctor, his advice was to give us all a teaspoon of brandy at bedtime to help us sleep!

Life was hard in the 1950s, as the UK economy was still recovering from the war, so one would have thought any additional help would have been greatly appreciated and welcomed with open arms. Some help came in the form of a letter, written to Mam, from the Keeper of the Privy Purse (the head of finance in The Queen's household!) containing a donation of £3.00, known as the King's or Queen's Bounty (see next page).

Her Majesty's Rule Regarding Triplets.

A short time ago a Mrs Ward, of Sheffield, gave birth to three children, all of whom subsequently died. An application for the usual Queen's bounty was made, and the following reply has been received:—"Lieut.—General Sir Henry F Ponsonby presents his compliments to Mr Thomas Collier, and with reference to his application on behalf of Mrs Ward, has to acquaint him that the Queen sometimes gives £3 to the mothers of three children at a birth, but only when the children all survive, or at any rate live long enough to cause expense, and when the parents are respectable but too poor to meet the unforeseen demands for providing for them at once without some little assistance. Any such donation is simply an act of charity on the part of the Queen, and is only granted to those who are in poor and indigent circumstances. If the case referred to comes within these conditions Sir Henry Ponsonby will submit it for Her Majesty's consideration on receiving the usual formal certificates of the birth and present existence of the children in question, together with an intimation from Mr Thomas Collier that the case is thoroughly deserving in every respect." In the present case the husband was in receipt of good wages, and in addition he was entitled to over £4 from a club on the death of a child. As he had three deaths, he claimed three times the funeral money, and under these circumstances Mr Collier could not certify he was "in poor and indigent circumstances." The wife has had five children within twelve months and seven in two years—twice twins and triplets. She is 25 years of age.

Daily Gazette, September 1880

It was formerly customary for the Sovereign to dispense a bounty to parents on the birth of triplets. During Queen Victoria's reign a gift of £3 for triplets and £4 for quadruplets was presented to the family when the children all survived: the parents being respectable but too poor to meet the unforeseen demands for providing for them all at once.

Details of the above process are in the Appendix at the back of this book.

Applications were sent to the Keeper of the Privy Purse who would reply asking for a letter testifying to the authenticity of the case from a doctor, clergyman or the Registrar of Birth, Deaths and Marriages. The donation would be sent via one of the above people to the mother who would sign and return a receipt for the money.

However, after 1938 these conditions were abolished and the payment was seen as an honour which parents were privileged to receive from the Sovereign. This payment ceased in 1958 to be replaced with a message of congratulations from the Queen. This process continued until 1994. Mam later forwarded this special letter to Grandad Leo in Middlesbrough but he never received it as it "got lost" in the post.

Mam was a very private person, having only a few close friends, mainly living in Middlesbrough. So, more often than not, she would have remained at home caring for the three of us and no doubt felt quite isolated from the outside world. Her jobs would have seemed endless with 130 nappies to change and wash each week, the 84 bottles of formula milk to prepare each week, clothes to wash and three babies to bathe with only our Dad to help; it can't have been easy. The nappies were made of terry toweling (a pile fabric with uncut loops) which would have had to be scraped clean of solids, soaked in a bucket, put through the washer and finally put through the wringer that forced the water from the nappies. These would then be pegged on the line to dry!

With three hungry babies to feed, it must have been noisy if we all cried in unison. Mam would put a bracelet on the baby she had just fed to avoid the mistake of one of us missing a feed. Dad would often return home from work and take over our care and bathing us ready for bed. I can imagine Mam breathing a sigh of relief and collapsing into the nearest chair from exhaustion and sleep deprivation, with us waking every 3 hours for a feed.

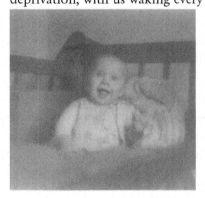

Dad told us of the time he had put us to bed as usual, but Gillian kept crying. He came into the bedroom and saw Frances had turned blue. He quickly scooped her up and ran a mile to the nearest public telephone. The Doctor came to give her medical treatment in the phone-box. Her life was saved by her sister that night.

On another morning he woke up to us crying and tried to open the door, but during the night I had bounced my cot across the door and it took him ages to gently push it out of the way without tipping me over.

Often as babies we were left to play together and were fascinated with thirty fingers and thirty toes. As we grew older, this could explain the reason we were found getting up to mischief! Mam did reveal that she sometimes left us sucking lollies with us watching her from the window as she nipped to the shops. A common practice in those days, although this would be frowned upon today.

Just before the Christmas of 1958 Dad inadvertently placed the last of his cigarettes on the coffee table. Our parents had just come back from shopping, buying a tin of corned beef for their Christmas Dinner. The packet of cigarettes was in easy reach of three inquisitive nineteen month old toddlers. He returned to find his three little darlings chewing his tobacco and licking coal. With no money left, he must have been very cross with us. Mam would have been about six months pregnant at this time. She was apprehensive about conceiving triplets again. What she didn't know was the odds of having identical triplets, conceived naturally, range from one in a million to one in two hundred million! A rare occurrence. Identical triplets are always the same sex and have the same blood group. Surely lightning wouldn't strike twice!

On 30th March 1959 Ann Elizabeth was born in hospital and much to her mother's relief she was the only one!

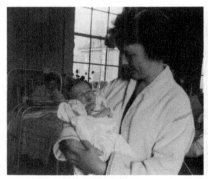
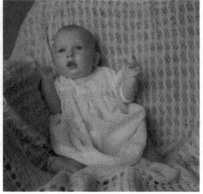

Usually Dad took time off work to care for us if Mam wasn't able to, but this time an "Aunty" came to hold the fort, remaining behind to take care of things. The only story we know of her is that she put our nappies, still covered in poo, straight into the washing machine! Dad returned from home from work to an awful stench permeating throughout the house and had to empty the washing machine in the garden and then clean everything up. Yuk!

So now our parents had four children under the age of two and this caused Mam to suffer with depression. There were no stories about additional support from the Catholic Church, but stories about the kindness of strangers who left suitcases of baby clothes on our doorstep. When Mam did venture out with the three of us in the big Silver Cross pram, people would place money underneath the covers and ask, "How do you tell the girls apart?" I've read that it can take up to two hours to get triplets ready for an outing and that it would take just as long to get to the shops because people wanted to stop and talk about us.

In most of our baby and toddler photos we look identical in our little dresses and cardigans; sitting with either Mam and Dad or with Grandad Leo on the grass. I guess they both would have helped prepare us for an adventure outside. Put back in the pram, we sat fastened in by our safety harnesses to ensure we didn't climb out!

We were always the centre of attention when walking in the Coventry streets or playing in the park with Grandad Leo. We must have been a handful, as one day Mam found we had managed to tip the pram forward to get to our baby sister, Ann. Thankfully she only slipped to the end of the pram and didn't fall out onto the concrete path! "You all probably thought she was a dolly", Mam said.

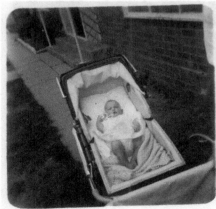

In the 1950s a mother would place her child on the potty when she thought the child needed to go to the toilet. If she got the timing right, the child would make the connection and learn to relieve themselves on the potty. This method worked, with ninety-five per cent of children being trained by eighteen months of age. As we would have been two years of age after Ann was born, I think it may have been in the following summer that Mam was more likely to have started training us. It makes sense as nappies would dry quicker and there would have been fewer clothes for us to take off! Did we each have our own potty, in a different colour, or would we have shared one? One thing is for sure Mam would have been highly motivated to get her three daughters trained and put in little pants as soon as possible! I had a nickname, Weewee, and hope it stemmed from Ann not being able to say Rosie when she was younger and not from lots of little "accidents".

At the beginning of 1961 Grandad Leo wrote to his daughter, Irene, to explain that a date for his marriage to Lily had been set for 24th July 1961. Lily was known to Grandad Leo, Grandma Audrey and Irene (my mum), as they patronized Skelton's grocery store. George R. Skelton, Lily's first husband, purchased this property in 1948 with every penny that they owned. Unusually for this time, the couple were both exempt from war service, as George had employment as a railway driver and Lily had a child under eight years of age.

Previously, during a bombing raid the railway station was targeted. The noise and shock of the attack caused George to fall on to the railway tracks. There was a train coming towards him and he was forced to tuck his arms by his sides as the train continued over his body, lying as still as he could in the gap. After suffering what is now known as Post-traumatic stress disorder (PTSD) George sadly committed suicide. Grandad Leo, himself a widower, continued to support Lily by purchasing his groceries from her store. This friendship began to grow, with Leo asking her out on a date to the Odeon Picture House. Over time this blossomed into a marriage of companionship, with both enjoying the game of Mahjong. This Chinese board game is very similar to the card game 'Rummy' and is a game of skill, strategy and calculation involving a game of chance.

After explaining the details of his future wedding, Grandad Leo told his daughter of his plans to move into Lily's flat, above the shop in St Barnabas Road, Linthorpe, after their wedding. This would leave Mam's family home at 7, Windsor Road empty, if she would like it for her family. Grandad, being very friendly with his Doctor, arranged to have medical cards set up in anticipation of their arrival. He never received a reply to his letter, so when a friend of Lily's heard it was available he offered to buy it. 7, Windsor Road was sold.

This turned out to be a disaster for us all, as I'll explain in the next chapter. It meant we had no home to go to when we fled from Coventry....

CHAPTER 4 – FINANCES

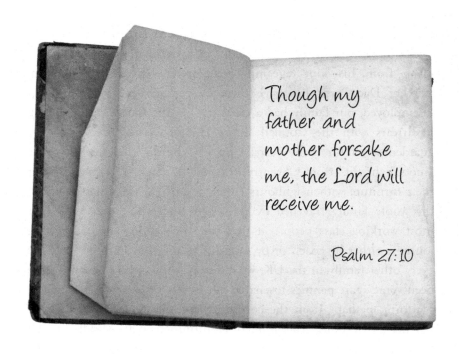

Though my father and mother forsake me, the Lord will receive me.

Psalm 27:10

The majority of women in the 1950s had roles mainly as wives and mothers, finding themselves taking care of the house and of their children. The husband was the main wage earner and was considered the head of the household in all matters, with the average wage being £10 a week at this time. Very few women worked and other than the state provided family allowance, which was paid directly to the mother, the ' housekeeping allowance' was at the discretion of the wage earner.

The culture in those days was that men thought it was their God-given right to spend time in the pub and would often be found after work drinking their precious wages away. Thirsty for a pint when their shift was finished, many of the clientele treated their "local" as a front room and would spend hours betting with cards, darts and dominoes. The public houses were open eight hours a day through the week and only five hours on a Sunday; so Dad may have wanted a break from his four screaming daughters. Whatever the reason, whether Dad spent his wage there or perhaps due to him being unemployed, our family had a crisis to face due to our parents being in arrears with the Council house rent. This has been a closely guarded secret for many years. Unpaid debt was the reason for the "moonlight flit" from Coventry to Middlesbrough. After sharing out their furniture with neighbours either side of 28 Mary Slessor Street, the whole family travelled by train back to Dad's hometown. Like most working class people at that time we would have taken long journeys either by coach or by rail, due to the fact that, like virtually every other family in the UK, we did not own a car. There must have been some spare pennies to enable our tickets to be purchased on the platform, perhaps from the contributions neighbours made for our parents' possessions? Travelling from Birmingham to Middlesbrough Station with four young children in tow, not to mention all the baggage, cannot have been an easy journey. Once on board, with the carriage gently swaying from side to side, I can only imagine Mam and Dad's relief as one by one we fell asleep. On arrival, a short bus trip from town to Linthorpe found us unannounced on Grandad Leo's doorstep at 7 Windsor Road.

This was on 13th July 1961. Word soon got round to family members who came to see, maybe for the first time, the triplets and Ann. It was remarked how well and healthy we all looked. Did they expect things to be different?

I now know that Mam must have received her father's letter and expected 7 Windsor Road to be still available for her family, no doubt causing her to think that the "moonlight flit" was the answer to escaping the debt, leaving it behind in Coventry. Apparently, she was very shocked to hear the news of the house sale and the truth was there was actually nowhere for her family to live. Her cousin, Alan, and his wife went home to discuss how they could help. They returned the following day to tell Mam she would never be homeless and volunteered to take her and Ann into their own home in Devonshire Road, which was just around the corner from her old home. They had limited space themselves having a young family of their own to care for. This same day Grandparents, Aunties and Uncles were asked to take part in a meeting to decide the way forward concerning our care. Uncle Jerry, Grandad George and Grandad Leo were furious with Dad, as his pride stood in the way of accepting financial help offered from his father-in-law. Raised voices and shouting could be heard throughout the house. Dad's behaviour led to his family being broken up and Grandad Leo refused to have his daughter's husband living under the same roof as him. Grandad Leo had no choice but to get in touch with a Father Dennett from the Middlesbrough Crusade of Rescue whose motto was:

"No Catholic child who is really destitute or whose faith is in danger or who cannot be otherwise provided for is ever to be refused."

This priest in turn referred us to the Sisters of Middlesbrough Nazareth House and we were taken there by the Welfare people just two days later, on the 15th.

Within forty-eight hours of arriving in our family's home town, we triplets had our bags packed yet again, in preparation for being moved on and placed into the hands of total strangers. I now know that this act, undertaken and agreed by the adults in our little world, caused a trait within me to be suspicious of peoples' intentions towards me. It is only recently that I have had the understanding of the far-reaching effect this has had on my life, resulting in me making the decision to forgive EVERYONE involved, to no longer be encumbered with this memory and being able to live the remainder of my life free from past influences and the rags of my childhood.

On admission to Middlesbrough Nazareth House we were given our entry numbers of 2780, 2781 and 2782. We were late arrivals and screamed the place down. Sister Joseph had us taken upstairs to the nursery, where we were handed over to Sister Mary. The home was full that night, resulting in us falling asleep in three little Z-beds.

Middlesbrough Nazareth House, 1906
'Catholic Orphanage and House of the Aged Poor

Nazareth House, Middlesbrough, 1964

Chapel

Nursery School

Middlesbrough Nazareth House took in homeless children, but was a place to which parents threatened to send their young family if faced with naughty or misbehaving children. Families would pass the home to visit Albert Park and no doubt this building would look dark and imposing through the eyes of a child, making this threat very real.

There are a few stories in our family history about the origin of Middlesbrough Nazareth House. The first one being that the property in Park Road North was bequeathed to the Nuns by a widow after the death of her husband. The second being that this was the only and original house to open its doors in 1884 for the aged and poor or homeless children.

After nearly a year of research I understand the facts to be as follows:-

June 1880: The Mother Mary Superior General (of the Nativity Owen) and the Mother Mary De Chantal arrived in Middlesbrough to open the new Middlesbrough Nazareth House at 17, Queen's Terrace, Queens square in the town. Middlesbrough Nazareth House was registered in the Catholic Mission book in 1880.

November 1880: A planning application was submitted by George Goldie, a renowned ecclesiastical architect, to include additional extentions to the above property.

June 1981: The Sisters of Nazareth rented the adjoining property, 15, Queens Terrace.

January 1884: The Mother General visited Middlesbrough and purchased a new house just built in Albert Park Road at the cost of £2400. Please note the correct address is Park Road North. This payment was given to a Mr William Imeson who owned this park villa.

May 1884: The Sisters and residents moved into this property, listed as a large mansion in own grounds opposite Albert Park.

1889: The adjoining house was purchased in Park Road North and the two houses made into one. Records are held in the Teesside Archives of planning permission to change two semi-detached dwelling houses (Park Villas) into a Roman Catholic school/orphanage. These were submitted by Edward Goldie, George's son.

1905/1906: The larger establishment was built side by side, next to the original building, and was certified for 78 Catholic children from various workhouses in the Diocese.

March 1907: Building work continued to this date with Middlesbrough Nazareth House being able to accommodate 206 children.

1984: The orphanage was closed and the children left. It later reopened in the year as a residential home for the elderly. By the turn of the century and beyond Middlesbrough Nazareth House had cared for 4,461 children and 1,187 elderly people.

2004: Middlesbrough Nazareth House finally closed.

Grandad Leo must have been overwhelmed with shock, knowing that he had just sold his home that was big enough for our whole family to live in, but he had no idea of our family life in the Midlands and that we would turn up the week before his wedding destitute. The wedding went ahead, as planned, on 24th July 1961.

Grandad Leo and Lily married at Sacred Heart Church and the reception was held at The Linthorpe public house. Mam moved into 7, Windsor Road for a very short time and happily attended her father's special day with Ann in tow. Our younger sister was two years old and for the first time drank out of a glass offered to her at the wedding reception. She bit down on the glass, breaking it, but thankfully wasn't injured.

After the house sale, Mam and Ann moved in with her cousin, Alan, in August 1961. Dad at first lived back in Pelham Street, then moved in with his brother, Ted, and his family, then later found accommodation in Southfield Road, near the town centre.

Mam settled in well, with the furniture passed on from her father being stored in the dining room. At first she began looking for rooms but soon lost interest as she was quite comfy where she was, thank you!

It was during this stay that Mam and Aunty Cecilia took our sister, Ann, to be baptized at The Holy Name of Mary church in Linthorpe Village on 8th September 1961. This was during the working week and Uncle Alan has no recollection of this event taking place.

Our parents had effectively separated and Aunty Cecilia refused to let Dad into her house when he came calling, being a strong supporter of her old school friend's wishes. A thaw began as she relented, inviting him to dinner on Christmas Day. Only Mam, Ann and Cecilia stayed, as Uncle Alan took his children to his in-laws.

In January 1962 Alan insisted that Mam move out and she found rooms in a terraced house with Dad and Ann.

During our stay in the orphanage Mam's entitlement to family allowance would have ceased, as we were no longer in her care. Family Allowance was a five-shilling a week payment given to parents only for their second and subsequent children. It had its origins in Post-War Britain, when the Government tried to ease the burden on families suffering amid housing shortages and food rationing, also to encourage more births to help increase a depleted population.

As Mam had a deep-seated fear of the Roman Catholic priests and nuns she consequently never came to visit us in the Home, whereas Dad occasionally collected us to take us to play in Albert Park and from time to time to the beach to play with our cousins.

Visiting was discouraged by the Nuns, as they would then be left to cope with the aftermath of upset children.

Maybe Grandad Leo heard gossip in his grocer's shop about 5, Mary Ann Street being up for sale.

It was one of nine terraced houses in a cul-de-sac off Linthorpe Road, only a few minutes walk away from St Barnabas Road. Mam ended up asking her father for the £300 to purchase it, believing this to be the only way to get her family back together again.

The houses on Mary Ann Street were nearly a hundred years old. Earlier records state that from 1851-1857 Isaac Sharpe operated a brickyard in Mary Ann Street, helping with major developments in New Linthorpe. The street was believed to have been named after the Reverend's daughter. Originally a Primitive Methodist Chapel opened in 1863 at the corner of the street, then, after it was sold in 1897, the congregation moved into the Temperance Hall at the other end of the cul-de-sac and it later became the Apostolic Church.

What our parents didn't know was that our new home was earmarked as part of the Council's housing programme. Already condemned, it was included in the 1950s post- war slum clearance plan of areas close to the town centre.

CHAPTER 5 – FEAST OR FAMINE

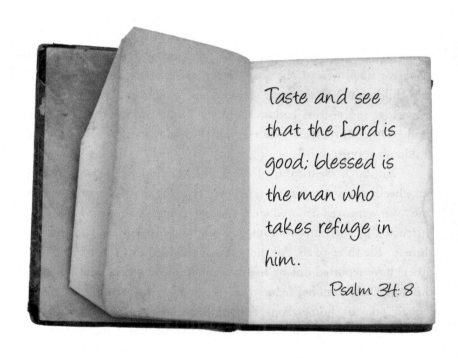

Taste and see that the Lord is good; blessed is the man who takes refuge in him.

Psalm 34: 8

During our year-long stay in Middlesbrough Nazareth House our care would have been funded either by the Crusade of Rescue or by the Local Authority. One of the good things about our stay was that all the children were well fed. We were given porridge (made with water), bacon, eggs and black pudding for breakfast, polony and other meat and vegetables for dinner. A scarce treat, fruit was only given at Easter, Christmas and when provided by visitors along with additional gifts of sweets and clothing. We were "better fed than outsiders", some say.

The short collection of our memories during this time are: getting bathed together in a big yellow bathroom (with Dad washing our hair; a dog was washed in the same bath), of ladies cleaning the floors in the building, being in separate beds in the dormitory when the three of us had chickenpox, getting the bus to school, our teddies being placed out of our reach on to the window ledge and lastly the pervasive smell of carbolic soap. Sisters, lay staff or older girls from the children's home would have been responsible for our care. Inspectors and visitors had access to the home and in April 1962 the Home Office Inspectors were very satisfied with the nurseries and the children's rooms.

Although identical triplets we all had distinctive personalities. I was cheeky (in a cute way), Francy was very shy and Gilly was a quiet one. We were well-behaved and obedient, always doing as we were instructed by the nuns without question and Sister Mary had taken a shine to the three of us. All these things shielded us from trouble that others have reported during life in a children's home. Maybe added to this was Dad's bull-headedness in insisting he was coming back one day to take us home. Ann Fothergill has written a book entitled "Memoirs of a Nazareth House Girl" giving a detailed account of her thirteen years' experience of living in the orphanage. Her book highlights the fact that not all children lived the same experiences within those four walls. During the years of 1947 to 1967 some children may have found themselves being shipped to Australia, being told they were going on holiday where the sun always shines. It was cheaper to deport them than to care for them on British soil. Some suffered the harshest treatment, with only a few doing well for themselves. That said, our experience in Middlesbrough Nazareth House was as a place of safety and God's best for the three of us during the early 1960s.

Parents and friends were clearly permitted to visit us, as our earliest memories were of Aunty Katie and Uncle Les who would come to visit us in their van. (Aunty Katie was Dad's sister and both she and their other sister, Mary, were unable to have children.) Les would wait outside as Katie nipped in to drop off shoes or clothes, three sets of each all in the same size and colour. This apparently upset the rest of the Farrow families who were also struggling to make ends meet and had hungry mouths of their own to feed!

There is a letter dated 12.11.2014 from the Sisters of Nazareth General Archive in the appendix, detailing further information about what went on during our time there

It felt amazing to be holding a letter revealing unexpected knowledge of Middlesbrough's Nazareth House's past and our earlier years!

After securing the property at 5 Mary Ann Street, Mam and Dad set about preparing their new home and slowly but surely began to fill it with the lovely furniture passed on from Grandad Leo. How happy Uncle Alan and Aunty Cecelia must have been to have all of those items removed from their dining room! Their growing family rearranged themselves, moving into different bedrooms, enabling them all to sleep upstairs once again.

On the 7th July we were "returned" to our parents.

There was no strict protocol for this discharge event. Often children were collected by their parents from Middlesbrough Nazareth House or someone from the Crusade of Rescue may have returned the children home. There has never been a case where a Sister was involved in this protocol. (see letter dated 26.10.2015 in appendix 4)

Our new home address had a door that led straight off the street into our front room. With net curtains up at the window, it looked quite dark. There was a table under the window, covered in a fancy doily (a small ornamental napkin). The fireplace was directly in front of you, with chairs close by to catch the warmth that radiated when the fire was lit. The next room was smaller with a bath in it. This had a hard cover over it and was used as a worktop, not for bathing in. Walking straight through led to the kitchen. There was a sink on top of bricks on the right near the window, with a housekeeper's dresser on the left. If you didn't have a pantry with a cold shelf, women would store the butter, milk and cheese in this – a refrigerator would have been unthinkable. At the end of the kitchen was a door leading to a small back yard. In the yard there was the outside privy, or toilet, next to a shed and a coal bunker. Stairs in the house led to two small bedrooms. Our room only had a double bed in it for the three of us to sleep in. I personally have no recollection of being "returned" and have now come to understand that the regime, routine and buildings were all very similar to those we had experienced in Middlesbrough Nazareth House.

We had previously travelled from Middlesbrough Nazareth House to a school, near St Mary's Cathedral, Our Lady of Perpetual Succour, on a double-decker bus. (The Cathedral, originally built on Sussex Street, was burnt down on 30th May 2000 and replaced by the current one in Coulby Newham.) The older girls would have walked there. They would set off in a group of three and have their underarms nipped by the Sister if they misbehaved! Our new school, St Philomena's, was on Ayresome Street and could only be reached by crossing Linthorpe Road. Mam would walk us part of the way, leaving us to cross this busy road with the Lollipop Lady or Man who would temporarily stop the flow of traffic, allowing us to cross over safely.

As we grew a bit older, a girl called Mary Payne collected us and walked us to school. Her mother was our Reception teacher who would sometimes give us all a lift home in her Mini. She was very kind to us, knowing about our time in Middlesbrough Nazareth House. She herself had a large family of nine children and each year before Christmas would have them all sort toys and clothes to be loaded in a trunk to be delivered for the children in the orphanage. Thank Heaven for the kindness of strangers again.

In 1963 our Church & school were renamed 'Sacred Heart'. Our younger sister, Ann, was 4 years old at this time and she recalls Mam telling the story of how she would sit on the stairs or the step waiting for her three older sisters to return home from school. Ann would be talking to her imaginary friend, Robin Hood. She was a "pesky" little sister, but remembers doing almost everything with the three of us.

As triplets we were identical and the teachers gave us name tags to help tell us apart. We had fun changing chairs and tags around when the teacher wasn't looking, often causing confusion within the classroom. I remember an incident where the teacher had the three of us stand and asked us to spell the colour 'white'. To our embarrassment and shame, not one of us got the spelling correct. Maybe we had been misbehaving that day, but this incident was witnessed by our peers, causing us to blush at this unwanted attention. We had experience failure while performing a relatively easy task causing me to grow to adulthood always wanting to be right. I now know it's OK to make mistakes and not always be right because I'm not perfect.

Most women shopped every day at the local bakers, butchers and greengrocers looking for the cheapest products and Ann would have had to go with Mam on these little excursions. Although money was still in short supply, with Mam waiting each Tuesday for the Family Allowance, we were always well fed with stews and hot meals. The least favourite of these meals was Panackelty. It was a favourite dish of the working class families in the North East of England though and consisted of layers of corned beef, potatoes and onions cooked in a stock. It was left to cook slowly throughout the day enabling women to continue with their housework. Mam would add tomatoes to this dish and it always had runny gravy. Yuk! But we would have to eat it, as there would be nothing else to fill our hungry tummies.

There is one memorable day in our lives when we had cornflakes for breakfast, dinner and tea! This was fact, even though we as children had hazy recollections of it happening more often. Mam was always slim, just eating the smallest amounts, probably doing without so she could feed us. I am grateful that Mam wanted us all to be together as a family again, even though she suffered hardship and had to sacrifice her food to keep our tummies fuller.

At the top of Mary Ann Street was Linthorpe Road. Along this main road was a bakery run by a lady called Lucy Harrison, who was born in 1914 and died in 1978. The smells from this place would waft in the air drawing the hungry children to the back of the shop. Later in the day we would scramble up the wall in the alley way to eagerly wait for the shop lady to share the broken biscuits and unsold cakes between us scruffy urchins. Next to the bakery was T. Armstrong's, the pet shop. Our first budgerigar, nicknamed 'the budgie', was bought from this shop. I remember him escaping from his cage near the window and flying straight into the coal fire. Thankfully he landed on the ledge at the back. I tried to reach him by putting my hand in the fire but had to shout for Dad to come and rescue him. The poor bird was covered in soot but he soon recovered.

On the other side of the bakery further along the block was Winterschladen, the wine and spirit shop, that had a "stag" standing proudly on the roof. Although no longer an off-licience, the stag still overlooks Linthorpe Road. An imposing red-brick building, it was first known as the "Golden Hind".

Dad would often give us a note and several empty beer bottles that we would then hand in to the licencee and return hot-foot with Dad's refreshments. Although eyebrows might be raised nowadays, this was a common practice in the "olden days".

I took my job as the eldest child very seriously, although I was only a few minutes older than my sisters. Gilly, however, was Ann's spare "Mam", holding her hand when needed, keeping an eye on her and always telling her to keep up. Walking home from school one day Ann ran out from behind a parked vehicle just narrowly missing getting knocked down by a car, as Gilly had instinctively grabbed her by her hair to yank her back. As soon as we got home, I told Dad who threatened Ann with a spanking if she did it again. She did, but we didn't tell on her again and she only got her smacked bottom when she ran right out in front of Dad. A hard lesson. Poor Ann. She remembers waiting for her turn to go to the loo and, being bored, she began picking and peeling the old paint off the kitchen door. Then, leaving the mess on the floor, took her turn on the toilet and then went out to play. Later Dad called us all in and lined us up to find out the culprit. None of us spragged on her!

It wasn't always Dad who disciplined us. Mam would smack the back of our legs leaving bright red fingermarks, if we answered back or were cheeky. One day Dad returned from work to see Mam smacking Francy. My sister had come down the stairs reading a comic. Mam had foolishly left a box on the stairs ready to take up later, as mothers do. Francy accidently knocked it and out tumbled the beautiful crockery to the foot of the stairs. Only two pieces were left unbroken, which Mam picked up and threw at the wall in temper! We were always shouted at or smacked if we accidentally broke anything.

Living just off Linthorpe Road, there was a danger of being run over by the busy traffic. There was a constant buzz in the background of noise from town life that only stopped late at night and on a Sunday, only to begin again early Monday morning. Consequently, we played on the doorstep away from the main road just under our window, sometimes climbing the wall of the Beeline garage just opposite our front. I remember riding my bike with no seat on it, a proper tomboy, safe but restricted.

The house was cold, especially in the wintertime. Mam would spend time washing the black mould from the landing walls, only for it to reappear a few days later. At bedtime Dad would fill Lowcock's lemonade bottles with hot water and put them in our beds to keep us warm through the night. We would often wake to the frost and even ice on the inside of the windows. Once out of bed it was straight into our clothes as fast as we could, watching our warm breath condense in the cold air. Downstairs, once the fire was lit and the gas cooker was in use, it was a bit warmer. Toast would be made by holding the bread on a fork in front of the fire. It tasted wonderful. We had a rug in front of the fire and when it was moved little silverfish would scatter in all directions. This small insect was a silvery grey colour and could be found in attics and bathtubs as well as other places in the house.

The combination of mould, soot, gas fumes and Dad's cigarette smoke created health problems in the family, especially for Gilly. She often had tonsillitis and bronchitis and Francy often suffered from earache. One of Doctor Strachan's earliest recorded visits to our home was 19th January 1963. I remember volunteering to lift my top so he could sound my chest. I had a cough with a rash and was diagnosed with measles. My next appointment was dated 20th October 1965, which makes me think I was more robust than my triplet sisters.

Perhaps my strong constitution was aided by eating sweets and the other 'treats' dropped by litterers on to the pavements. One such memory was of being in Linthorpe Rest gardens, over the road from home. Oddly, I was by myself, as Dad always sent us out in twos. These gardens had been laid out by the Council Parks Department in 1954 and had several teak benches donated as gifts for memorials to important men of that time. It was Winter and, as I walked through the freshly fallen snow, I spied a piece of chewed gum near my shoe. I picked it up, thinking the snow was clean and the gum frozen and, after coming to the conclusion it was safe to eat, popped it in my mouth. Francy also recalls picking up frozen peas to eat from the floor in the local supermarket, Hinton's.

Eh, we were hungry, scruffy children and to add to our misery our shoes would often be worn out with holes in the soles. The cornflake box came in handy as shapes were cut out to put inside our shoes. We often had wet feet and Gilly remembers feeling very scruffy and poor as we knelt down in Church, thinking people would see the holes in her footwear. If we whispered or giggled the old ladies in the pew behind would poke us in the back with their bony fingers to shush us, but all it served to do was make us giggle more. They must have thought they were "Pew-holders"! However poor we might have been, we nevertheless felt that God's hand was still upon our lives. There was an Apostolic Church at the far end of our road and a lady called Chris would walk past us playing in the street and pray for us.

The famine was to turn to a feast during our teenage years when dad began to travel to Saudi Arabia, sub-contracting for a company in the United Kingdom.

CHAPTER 6 - FAITH AND FESTIVALS

Dear children
keep yourselves
from idols.

1 John 5:21

Although my three sisters and I have travelled through the same upbringing, some memories of our past are more clearly held in one individual's mind than in the others'. Our memories of faith and festivals have been assembled into the following narrative.

The first place the three of us were encouraged to learn about the Roman Catholic religion would have been during our time spent in Middlesbrough Nazareth House. We would have been taught to say "simple" prayers like The Lord's Prayer and The Hail Mary. Then from school age, at five, we would have had to attend Mass, held each day in the orphanage's chapel. After leaving the Home in July 1962 we began to attend Mass at Sacred Heart Church, as this building was just around the corner from our house on Linthorpe Road. Sometimes you would be asked at school if you had been to Church the previous day. It was really in your best interests to say truthfully that you had. Although the Apostolic Church was at the bottom end of our road we couldn't go there, as it wasn't Catholic.

The four of us were made to attend Mass every Sunday even though Mam and Dad didn't go. Mam would sometimes decorate on that sacred day and the Priest would say people would go to Hell for doing that.

Entering Church by the side door, we would place our black lace veils (mantillas) on our heads as a sign of respect then dip a finger into the holy water held in the tall marble font and make the Sign of the Cross. Walking quietly to the pew we would genuflect, rapidly dropping to one knee and immediately rising again, before taking our seats. If we were early we sat at the front of the Church but mostly, due to being late, we sat at the back.

The Church was cold and draughty. If you wanted to take Communion you had to miss breakfast. Most of the service was in Latin, so it was boring for us children. The monotony was broken as we went to the altar to take the Eucharist, kneeling once again to reveal our holey shoes to the world.

Church was a mysterious place and, as children, you would look around in wonder at the "Stations of the Cross", the pictures, the plaques and the statues. Some made you feel sad. There were confessional boxes, used once a week on a Saturday where people would confess their sins to the Priest, who was behind a wooden mesh. This was to stop him from knowing who that person was, but surely he would recognize the voice? Usually only children attended this sacrament, along with a few adults. Our parents stayed away. Even at that young age, I remember thinking there were rules for children and different ones for the grown-ups. A case of do what I say, not what I do. Maybe it was due to the fact that the Priest would give a punishment of reciting the Our Father or Hail Mary five times or more, depending on what "sins" you had committed. Sometimes Gilly would feel she had to make some up.

We took our Fist Holy Communion in 1965 and had to learn about the Catechism before we were allowed to be confirmed at around seven years of age (actual date 31.1.65). This taught us the first principles, or basics, of the Roman Catholic faith and also taught us how to play our part in the Sacrament of Confirmation.

Each year we would take part in the Corpus Christi and the May procession. My sisters and I have fond memories of these events, probably because it was one of the few occasions that our white dresses were brand new. Sister Joseph had them hand made by a Mrs Tester, our schoolmate Tony's mam, and no doubt helped towards the cost. This Sister helped our Mam with clothing us by bringing secondhand clothes round to the house that were always too big! The 31st May was a Devotional Day in which the statue of the Virgin Mary would be carried through the streets of Middlesbrough and then on to the Cathedral. We wore our white dresses with pride and would join the hundreds of young people from other Catholic schools, together singing praises and saying prayers. The girls would throw petals, with well-wishers and proud parents lining the streets, cheering.

In our early years we simply accepted Church and family traditions, innocently regarding these ceremonial acts and rites as everyone's way of life.

We loved to sing, having a gift of quickly picking up a tune or melody without being able to read music. We found ourselves joining

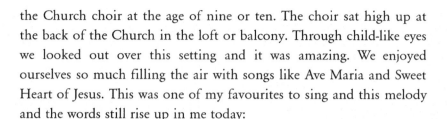

the Church choir at the age of nine or ten. The choir sat high up at the back of the Church in the loft or balcony. Through child-like eyes we looked out over this setting and it was amazing. We enjoyed ourselves so much filling the air with songs like Ave Maria and Sweet Heart of Jesus. This was one of my favourites to sing and this melody and the words still rise up in me today:

"Sweet Heart of Jesus
Make us know and love Thee
Unfold to us the treasures of Thy grace
Oh, touch our hearts, so cold and so ungrateful
And make us Lord
Thy own for evermore
Sweet Heart of Jesus we implore
Oh, make us love Thee more and more"

Apparently the words above are from 2 different verses!

This Roman Catholic Church commenced in a temporary building in Ayresome Street near the school. The parishioners moved to Sacred Heart Church on Linthorpe Road early in 1932. The stained glass windows that we could see directly above the Altar, from the balcony, had been donated by Church members and were installed mainly during the 1960s. There were nineteen beautiful windowpanes around the building depicting scenes from the Bible: The Crucifixion, the Sacred Heart, the Raising of Lazarus, the Good Shepherd and Christ with the Children, to name but a few. I remember the sunshine streaming through the windows, which produced a rainbow of colours into the Church setting, lighting on the parishioners below. Beautiful.

Occasionally Father Crowley or one of the Priests would pay the family a visit, sometimes staying for a dram or a wee bit of whisky. Despite the temptation to share a glass or two with this important visitor, Dad would disappear upstairs and not come down again until this visitor had left. Our Dad had learned the hard way and knew the Priest would try to encourage him to attend Mass and aim to convert him to Catholicism. A neighbour three doors away would rush to put their budgie into the kitchen when they heard the Priest knocking at their door. She had taught it to say "You are a naughty little bugger!" and she didn't want that type of language repeated to the holy father.

Mam would be left to cope with any questions put to her, maybe, "When are you going to attend Mass again?" or "Do you have any spare money to put in the basket?". I wonder if Mam was reminded that the Catholic orphanage had supported her in her time of need, therefore making her feel obliged to return the favour. Whatever the reason, Mam and Dad had a fear of the Priests and Nuns that spilt over into our everyday lives. I remember living in fear of men most of the time, especially if my triplet sisters were not around.

Life outside of Church and home was also a mix of fear and enjoyment. I remember sheltering under the Stag doorway with my sisters, afraid of the thunder and lightning overhead, afraid of playtime at school as a boy called Dennis would punch me in the tummy, afraid of the Grey Lady (a ghost) that lived in the cellar, afraid of "Nitty Nora the head explorer" who was employed in searching out the small insects or eggs in your hair. Mam had four daughters, all with long hair, so I remember it being a fairly common occurrence for one of us to have nits. In those days we would be sent along the road to the clinic to have a yellow solution put on our hair, then Mam would spend time using a metal comb to get rid of the little critters. I was afraid of fire, dogs, the dentist and the graveyard. Was that a common experience for children growing up in the 1960s?

I remember one warm July morning, the sun and the light disappeared behind a wall of thick cloud. Then the heavens opened. I felt very scared as the teachers hurried us all back into our classrooms. No one explained what was happening, making it a very unsettling experience. I now know this to have been " The Day of Great Darkness", as written in the Gazette live dated 2.7.1968. This killer storm battered Teesside at 11.40am on 2nd July 1968, turning the sky black, as thunder, lightning & hailstones (the size of gobstoppers) rained down on the area for miles around. People prayed for deliverance from the great blackness & dropped to their knees in prayer in the town centre, thinking it was the end of the world. Traffic came to a standstill & rivers of rain caused the manhole covers to lift & spout like whales! I remember it being hot & humid after the storm had passed.

Through all these experiences our behaviour was kept in check. We were always "good girls". One precious memory of the benefits of being a good girl was when Sister Joseph called me to her office to reward my good behaviour with a new set of rosary beads. Rosary means "crown of roses" and this is used as a form of prayer, especially in the Catholic religion. I was so happy and pink with excitement to receive such a special gift, eagerly waiting to go home to show my parents.

Maybe we were so well-behaved because we didn't want to be sent back to Middlesbrough Nazareth House, but more likely it was the "God" we knew who was "all-seeing" and "all-knowing" who produced that effect on us. Added to this, as teenagers, Dad would always know where we were and what we were up to. Just like God. The simple explanation here was that his friends were reporting back to him that they had seen us out and everyone knew us! I think there was only one other set of triplets in the area. They lived in Redcar. They were boys; so no confusion there then!

Anthony aged 3/35

Our cousin, Anthony (Alan and Cecelia's eldest boy), often called for us on the way to Sacred Heart School. He remembers 5, Mary Ann Street as a small, neat place. A bit old-fashioned, but pretty and tidy with lacy cotton covers on the tables in the parlour. The toilet out the back had a broken cistern and needed flushing with a bucket. He remembers standing in our front room at 9 years of age telling Mam that the local newsagent had agreed he could have a paper round once he was old enough. This to him was a definite job offer much to Mam's amusement!

We remained in Mary Ann Street until October 1967 with the time approaching for these nine single terrace houses to be knocked down. This took the form of a Compulsory Purchase Order, which allows certain bodies, like the local Borough Council, to obtain land or property without the consent of the owner. Four other families remained, until in 1969 these homes were demolished, along with the Apostolic Church.

I understand our parents received about £150 (the amount the land was worth) and presume this princely sum was returned to Grandad Leo. I always thought our land made way for the Beeline Bus Company development, but apparently not, as the Beeline Roadways had the depot there prior to 1959.

The Council offered our family a house on Cumberland Road Estate less than a five minute walk from our old one. This house was part of Linthorpe's largest area of post-second World War housing, finally completed in 1952.

I have a very clear recollection of walking through the front door of 19, Hereford Close and standing still in the empty sitting room. Looking around I could see and smell that the walls had recently received a coat of paint. Not a damp black patch of mould in sight, making it a clean and sunny room. It was amazing! We were moving into a property that had three bedrooms, an inside toilet and bathroom as well as an outside loo! Our new home was like a palace. Running from room to room led us to the large garden out the back with a separate wash-house. The icing on the cake was that all these properties faced a large green and, although there was a road running through the centre of the green, there was only one exit making the cul-de-sac a safe, child-friendly space in which we could run and play. This house move proved to be a life-changing event for the whole family.

CHAPTER 7 – FUN

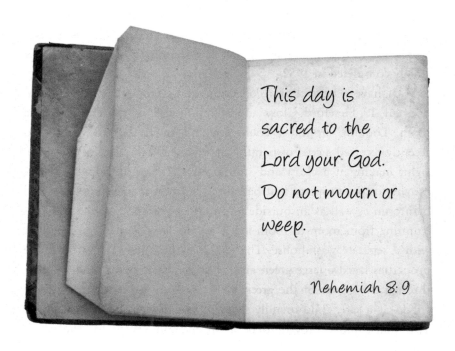

This day is
sacred to the
Lord your God.
Do not mourn or
weep.

Nehemiah 8: 9

Thus began a more settled period in our upbringing; with life being a whole lot better, in fact full of fun and games. After the constraints and limits of Mary Ann Street with its busy traffic, Mam and Dad appeared more relaxed with us and altogether more at ease now we were living in Hereford Close. I clearly remember waking up in the front bedroom to the birds singing sweetly in the tree and peace seemed to have settled on our new home. Not one of us remembers the actual event of changing residence, even at ten years old! The actual moving of our furniture was probably done whilst we were in school. We would have been reminded of our new address that morning before setting off, or perhaps Dad collected us from school?

A neighbour, Pat, remembers our family causing quite a stir in the Close. People could be heard saying, "Have you seen the triplets? They are identical and gorgeous." Asked for her recollections for this book, Pat describes fond memories of listening to the three of us laughing as we played out on the green. Joyful and happy to be in each other' company, she remarked we were always dressed alike and she remembers commenting, "They should be in modelling". Dressed in white tops and dogtooth trousers or pedal-pushers, our clothes always matched. Even Grandad Leo bought us matching outfits of blue dresses (in different shades of blue) and red and white zigzag-patterned jumpers. Poor Ann always had hand-me-downs, in fact, three of everything!

On another occasion, Pat remembers us all running to meet her after she returned from the shops. As she pushed her pram we all pressed forward for a turn to take the newest baby around the Close. Bonny, blonde girls, good at sharing and taking turns. Sometimes we would all knock on her door to walk her son, Mark, holding his hands and mothering him until he was old enough to race around the green with us.

Our days were filled with skipping or playing wildly with the other children in our road, especially the boys. They had a tough time trying to beat us girls at Kerby, Marbles and Cannon.

Kerby was a game played with a football. Two opponents faced each other on opposite kerbs, then they would take turns trying to hit their opponent's kerb with the ball. You scored points by hitting the kerb cleanly which made the ball bounce back for you to catch. The first to twenty won.

Cannon was played with a can, a tennis ball and lollysticks. The can was placed within a chalk circle on the road and the sticks placed on top. Two teams played. The object of the game was to roll the ball and knock the can over. Your team would then try to place all the sticks back on top of the can to win. But the opposing team would try to chuck the tennis ball at you to take you out of the game. It involved a lot of racing around the green. The winners shouted "Cannon!".

Our favourite game was marbles and we had a white stool with a hollow seat, kept in the "washey" (our name for the outhouse), to keep all our winnings in. It was a game of skill. The marbles had different names like glassies, steelies, blueies and bongies. All were different in size and colour. The children would roll or throw the marbles into a shallow hole in the ground or use the nearest mucky manhole cover. Other marbles could be knocked out of the way using bottlies (big glass marbles). Our state of happiness often depended on how full or empty the stool was!

Girly games were hop-scotch, twoey-ball, skips, cats cradle using wool or elastic with our hands or feet, pick-up-sticks and handstands. We would play on the step with our dolls, either being Mams and Dads or Doctors and Nurses. We were very innocent and, as children, made our own fun and knew no bounds in our vivid imaginations! Our shrieks of delight would resound around the close, especially when we girls beat the boys at their own games. Girls and boys of all ages (especially from 5 years old up to 15 years) played out together and would go en masse to the park with Dad, who liked to organize football matches for us all. When dusk arrived, the older children would start telling scary stories to the younger ones.

During the 1960s sweets saw a boom as sugar rationing had only ceased a decade before. We would sometimes go to Grandad Leo's grocery shop and he would treat us, allowing us to pick our own sweets. Some would be weighed, like cherry lips, aniseed balls or Yorkshire mix, but I preferred a packet of Spangles. These were square boiled sweets with the old English flavours like liquorice, mint-humbug, pear drop, aniseed and treacle. Other favourites were Rowntrees' fruit gums, Love Hearts, Toffo, Smarties, gum balls and gobstoppers. Sometimes in summer we went to a newsagents a couple of streets from St Barnabas Road to buy ice-lollies. We would quickly

eat these, as sometimes one of the sticks had written on it "free lolly"!
We would claim our free one and share it between the four of us.

I remember another
"sweetie" incident happening in
Albert Park one day. As
children we would run through
the park, going in and out of
the bushes, but this time there
was a man offering some little
girls sweets. Dad told us to stay

together as he rescued the girls and ran after the man. When he came
back we went looking for the Park Keeper to tell him of the "nasty"
man.

We were encouraged to get out from under our mother's feet, so
we would be found running around in the fresh air most of the day.
This made for hungry children, but we would have to wait to be called
in for tea. Our house had a strict rule of "asking permission" to take
any food from the pantry or cupboard. The only exception was
Christmas.

The best religious festival of the year was celebrating Christmas
Day, to remember the birth of Jesus Christ. It is a holiday season with
customs including gift-giving, exchange of cards, advent calendars,
Christmas tree lights, church services and a special meal: Christmas
Dinner. For children especially, Christmas morning involved waking
very early to see if Father Christmas had "left" any presents. As young
girls we awoke to find a sack (pillowcase) of gifts each, left at the foot
of our beds. We would sneak downstairs in our nighties then choose a
chair to sit on. Having our backs to each other we would dip our
hands into our pillowcases and shout out the shape of the present, so
we opened the same "one" together. One special gift was a plastic
dolly. We each had one but their hair was a different colour. Mine had
dark brown glossy hair and I still have her in the loft, so she's over 50

years old. Sometimes we got knitted rag dollies sewn lovingly together by Mam at night when we were all in bed, with the insides stuffed with her old tights. Some other gifts we would have received were skipping ropes, board games like Monopoly or Snakes and Ladders, jigsaws. dress-up doll books, Enid Blyton books of the Famous Five or The Secret Seven, bobbins with nails on the end to wind wool around, Fuzzy Felt, Spirographs and clacker balls (two hard balls on string attached to a stick which swung gently up and down to cause the balls to bang against each other faster and faster). Then when you got to the end of the presents, there was always an orange, red rosy apple and chocolate coins to finish off with! Ann remembers getting essentials such as knickers, socks, nighties & slippers.

As children we would try to save the only pocket money we received, (though our younger sister remembers us often going straight to the shop to buy two comics and two rations of sweets to be shared between us all!). This money came from Grandad George on a Saturday night when he called, with Uncle Jerry and Uncle Ted ,to take Dad to the pub which was just around the corner from our home. Uncle Jerry would always scare us by chasing us upstairs, causing us to run squealing into the bathroom, locking the door behind us.

Dad's Christmas presents from us would be jellied sweets in a posh box and hard toffee in slabs with metal hammer. Mam's favourite chocolates were Black Magic that we always got her at Christmas. We remember buying her a velvet covered plastic deer ornament and a black & white coarse real fur purse , which may have been a birthday present from us all. She must have been touched as she gave us a hug, which wasn't very often, and they were kept like treasured possessions in her drawer upstairs. She often had a faint scent of Oil of Ulay and she had the warm smell of tea on her breath.

I was a tomboy and was often in more trouble than any of my sisters. Caught scrumping (stealing apples) from a neighbour's garden,

I was disciplined and made to go to my room. Maybe the reason I did it was to fill my hungry tummy. One time at the chip shop I got bored waiting for Mam to be served so I ventured down the alley. After pulling a cat's tail, I ended up with both sides of my face tram-lined with claw marks! Playing out on the green one day, I was bitten by the bad-tempered Dalmatian from over the road who had escaped his gate! But one of the worst situations I got myself into, was allowing myself to be taught how to swear like a trooper by an older girl in the Close. My parents were not happy and, after several instances of unacceptable behaviour involving my "friend", I was banned from going to her house and from playing with her. This sparked a noisy argument on our doorstep between our parents. Brave and feisty action from Gilly saved the day. She jumped on the man's back causing someone to shout, "You can't hurt the bairn!". This led to the situation calming down and the neighbours returned home.

As children we were expected to run errands for our parents. If children didn't do as they were asked back then, their Mother usually gave a verbal warning of, "Wait until your father gets home!". Being smacked on our legs was generally accepted as the way our Mam doled out her punishment to us children.

I was asked one day to go to the machine in Lancaster Road to get Dad his cigarettes. He was still in bed. It was a short trip to the top of the road and I was soon back with his favourite brand of Player's Navy Cut. I was told to light one off the gas cooker. On the way upstairs I took a quick puff, nearly falling back down coughing. Dad never said a thing and it put me off smoking for life, as it did Ann as well!

Although grateful to have escaped any temptation to take up smoking I was ironically addicted to Candy Cigarettes and Spanish Gold Tobacco! Candy cigarettes were made from a chalky sugar, wrapped and boxed in paper to resemble real cigarettes; some even had red tips to make them look like a lit one! Sweet tobacco was also known as Spanish tobacco and sweet baccy. This was delicious sweet coconut strips dusted in chocolate powder and wrapped in red and gold packaging just like the real tobacco in the pouch that Grandad George smoked. Some of the older children smoked their "sweet fags" until they were old enough to start smoking properly. They would have a quick puff and then quickly scoff the packet; but no lighting up or smoking the "sweet baccy" or you would end up looking a real idiot!

I remember bright sunny days where we girls would sit in the garden podding peas for tea-time. Splitting one side of the pod, we would remove the peas which hopefully made it into a pan! A real labour of love, especially if the pods were picked early in the season, producing small sweet peas. We would sit for hours on the green, together making daisy chains for our hair, wrists and necks. Such an innocent pastime. In late Summer we would go knocking on the neighbours' doors to ask permission to collect the rose petals gathering on the paths. We returned home to ask Mam for an old jam jar into which we placed the petals; water was added and the contents were mashed a lot to produce a brownish-red liquid. The petals were taken out leaving rose petal perfume. We would use it for a couple of days but it soon "went off" and ended up down the drain.

Occasionally Mam would take us to Albert Park, on warm sunny days, to go roller-skating on the artificial skating rink. After paying for the "proper" roller-skating boots she would sit on one of the tiers of wooden seats with a drink., almost certainly a cup of tea. As we practised this new challenge in life, she would be thinking, "They'll be covered in bruises." as we fell over, one by one! The sun would be setting, lighting up the sky in orange and reds, before we were tired enough to be persuaded it was home-time.

We had our own roller boots, though these only fastened with two straps over the top of our normal shoes, not with laces like the boots at the rink. Francy remembers fighting with a boy in the road over a pair that belonged to her. Normally shy, it was unlike her to fight, but she did and won! You had to be careful skating round the pavements in our close, as these were uneven, so most of the time we raced up and down the road, careful of any cars parked up. If there was any trouble with the families or children in the road our parents would be told these events four times over, with the three of us finishing each other's sentences. Our voices would get louder and louder in our excitement and need to be heard. Mam's and Dad's heads would go from side to side, a bit like watching a tennis match, until the full story unfolded. Mam, though, appeared to make more of a fuss of Ann, maybe due to the fact that she wasn't a triplet. She was also the youngest daughter and, as she grew older,had the same sense of humour as her mother. As far as the three of us were concerned, Ann was her favourite, whilst Gilly was often on the receiving end of Mam's unkind behaviour. Francy and I kept our distance, but it didn't stop us telling tales to Dad when he came in from work. To escape arguments between them we would disappear to the "washey" and come out again when our parents were friends once more.

Rightly or wrongly, I remember Mam always believing Ann's version of events, regardless if mine were true or not. Oh, the joys of family life!

CHAPTER 8 – FATHER

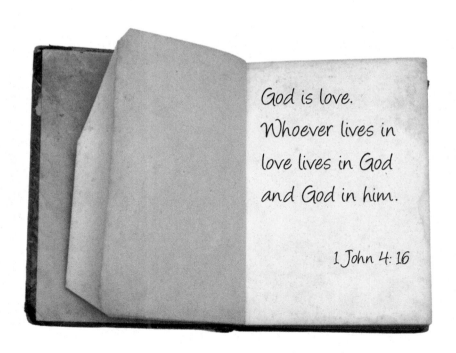

God is love.
Whoever lives in
love lives in God
and God in him.

1 John 4: 16

Our father was an electrician by trade and was one of the thousands of employees to work for Rediffusion Ltd. This business distributed radio and TV signals through wired relay networks to over a hundred and seventy-five towns in Great Britain, manufacturing its first television set in 1947 and by 1954 was the first commercial station to take to the air at home and abroad.

With differing versions surfacing in our individual memory banks, I have established that we were the first family in our cul-de sac to rent a TV, due to dad's work.

In the 1960s children's programmes were only broadcast for twenty hours a week, with a six o'clock curfew called the Toddlers truce. This would send our street friends home, as the black and white picture disappeared and the screen went blank. The British Broadcasting Corporation (BBC) placed an emphasis on educating and protecting the minds of their younger viewers. However, in 1955 ITV began to broadcast cartoons, adventure stories and westerns merging the line drawn between the different age groups. Much-loved entertainment from our 'goggle box' or 'telly' came from programmes such as Robin Hood, Flipper, Lassie, Andy Pandy, Basil Brush and The Flowerpot Men, with later favourites being Thunderbirds , The Flintstones and Captain Pugwash.

Dad would park his van either outside our house or on Linthorpe road. These white vans or cars had distinctive yellow stripes along the side of the vehicle, advertising the Reddiffusion company in black lettering within the stripes. There were only two seats in the front, as the back of the van contained TV sets, parts and tools needed for Dad to complete his work. If we were good girls, one of us was chosen to go for a ride around the block in it. Francy remembers it was more often me than her, even though she had been just as good! Maybe it could be perceived that I was Dad's favourite, even though Francy was more well-behaved than any of us. On opening the van's door a warm 'worky' smell would fill my nostrils and I would climb into the spare seat with a happy feeling in my heart. I definitely felt one of his special daughters, as did my sisters when it was their turn.

I have seen a letter from Rediffusion dated March 1968 in which the position as a trainee TV service technician was offered the wage of £13, 14 shillings a week. As money always seemed to be in short supply, it may have been one of many reasons that Dad decided to go to night school to complete his City & Guild's engineering course.

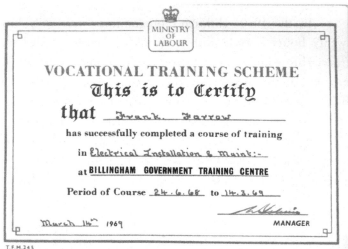

Dad explained this was a secret and not a word about it could be spoken to anyone. These new qualifications eventually enabled him to find employment with Haig & Ringrose, Wilton, Dorman Long and British Steel as a sub-contractor.

Without a car or the spare cash to fund trips further afield when off work or at weekends Dad would take us to the Dorman Museum or Albert Park and sometimes to both. We went so often that Mam became bored with it and she would, therefore, stop at home doing housework or, the hobby of the 1960s, knitting. Her task was to knit four pink cardigans and, although we saw lots of knitted sleeves and knitted fronts in her knitting bag, we never wore one as she never stitched or completed a whole top! It always reminded Francy of the fairytale of the "wild swans". A young Princess is tasked with the job of knitting shirts for her twelve brothers. A spell has turned them into black swans. This could only be broken if the shirts were made of sharp nettles, which cut her hands as she worked. She becomes mute as part of the bargain. A King from a faraway land falls in love with the mute Elise and she accepts his proposal. Now living in a room in his castle, she runs out of nettles to complete the shirts. She is seen picking nettles from the Church graveyard by the Archbishop who accuses her of witchcraft, sentencing her to death by burning at the stake. Elise continues to knit even as the executioner makes ready for her burning. Suddenly the black swans descend from heaven causing her to throw the shirts over her brothers and breaking the curse. They speak for their sister and the firewood takes root then bursts into flower. The King picks the top-most flower and they marry and live happily ever after. Interestingly, we never actually saw Mam knitting! It's a good job Mam wasn't tasked with saving us or we would have been done for!

On the way to the Museum we would pass a local sweet shop. Dad would stop and buy a quarter pound of sweets to share between us all. If Uncle Bill came to visit us, we could choose our own quarter of sweets off the high shelves at the back of the store. There was a small automatic bell hung above the shop door that sounded to warn the shopkeeper that he had a customer. He wasn't our favourite uncle, but we still took sweets from him. Children can be very mercenary.

As we stepped into the Dorman Museum we were greeted by a stuffed lion. We called him Leo, but he was the museum's adopted emblem – the A E Pease Lion. Then, off to the left, there was a clear plastic beehive, allowing visitors to see the bees at work in the hive. The queen bee had a bright yellow spot on her back making her easy to find. Francy would love to stand watching these "busy bees" for ages. We would go on to the Nelson Room which had stuffed birds in it. It had a smell, not an unpleasant one, which is not surprising as some of the birds were contributed by a Mr H W F Bolckow in 1874! This room also displayed the birds' eggs and nests that had been collected and donated by local people. Such a variety in the size and colour of this natural collection. We would frequently run ahead of Dad to hide in the next room, sometimes going behind the display cabinets. As we crouched close to the ground we could see the traps and rat poison, often being told off by any adults watching our antics. We spent hours wandering around this building looking at the works of art or other curiosities, especially if it was raining cats and dogs! Depending on the weather, we would buy a "creamy ice" from Rea's ice cream shop, then cross the main road again to go through the black wrought iron gates of the entrance to Albert Park. There was a walkway called the Wellington Walk that led straight down to the boating lake at the opposite end of the park. Our little family would meander past the weather gauge, the sundial, the tennis courts, the bandstand, the Rose Garden, the ornate fountain and the little railway as well as skipping and running behind the large horse-chestnut trees until finally reaching the eleven steps that led down to the boating lake.

Off to the right was the playground that held the scariest, highest slide around. As a child you had to be really brave just to climb all the steps leading to the top of it! Hopefully, your Dad would be waiting at the bottom in case you slid off the end. I remember a girl tumbling off. Dad rushed to catch her but she broke her arm in the fall and was rushed off to the General Hospital. After playing on the swings, Dad would take us for a treat on the boating lake. The vessel would rock gently from side to side, causing us to giggle and cling on tightly to the sides as we all clambered on board. How one of us never fell in the water, I'll never know! Each boat had a number and when your allotted time was up the male voice from the tannoy system would say, "Come in number seven". Sad-faced, we would row back to the boating house trying to avoid the ducks and swans with the oars. Back on dry land we would feed the birds with the "ducky bread", a favourite British pastime, with some of it finding its way into our hungry mouths.

Tired but happy, we would set off back home, taking the short cut through the gap in the iron railings on Park Road South. It was just near here where our first budgie had been buried in a shoebox. Lifting Ann onto his shoulders Dad would carry her for the rest of the journey home. When our little sister was tired, she would suck her thumb and for some reason had to be encouraged to eat her greens. Mam bought her a special plate with a house scene on it and Gilly would gently cajole her into eating the mashed potato, helping stab her peas and feeding her; so the man on the plate picture could get out of the house again and praising her when she had finished! In photographs she always looked shy and bashful with her little ears sticking out.

There was fun to be had in Albert Park whatever the season. In Spring the flowers would start to peep their heads out , like snowdrops and later on the yellow bloom of the daffodils. Summer was for picnicking and playing on the grass. Autumn was spent kicking through the dry leaves and Winter was spent collecting conkers. These prizes would be taken home. A hole would be made through the middle of the conker and a strong piece of string would be threaded through with a knot tied at one end to stop it falling off. We would have "conker fights" with the other children in the Close, hitting each other's conkers in turn until one was completely destroyed. Conkers can be known as cheesers, having one or more flat sides, due to sharing a pod with other conkers (twins or triplets!).

I remember Uncle Eric calling for us and taking us, with Dad, to go to see Bambi at the Majestic cinema. A trip to the cinema was a very rare occurrence until becoming an ABC Minor in later years! The film made me cry as Bambi's story unfolded of friendship, love and the miracle of life. The strange thing is neither of my sisters remembers going to see it! Dad's side of the family would often visit and we would spend many happy hours with our cousins frolicking in Albert Park.

Weekdays, however, were a different kettle of fish! Dad could be authoritative and very strict. If he shouted at us, we would all burst out crying. We were kept in to complete our homework and were not allowed to play outside if we didn't get all our spellings correct. Sometimes it seemed as if we could never please our parents or do well enough to make them proud. Whilst other children in the Close were allowed up late, we were put to bed early. Gilly would peep out of a narrow strip of curtain watching the other children playing around. Mam and Dad would get annoyed if they could hear us chattering away. Mam would shout up the stairs, "Are you girls asleep yet?". Gilly would jump back into bed causing us to giggle and duck under the covers.

Sometimes Dad would go to the pub after work and was always out at the weekend. He seemed to have a split personality after drinking, causing arguments on returning home. We could hear our parents shouting at each other through closed doors and would huddle together to wait for the storm to pass. As children we didn't understand that Mam suffered from depression and back then Mam and Dad probably didn't understand it either. Dad would say to her,

"Pull yourself together" and didn't entertain the thought that his behaviour added to Mam's misery. Maybe these arguments were caused by money worries. If Dad still went out drinking, he would have wanted to pay his own way, resulting in him spending more than he had to keep pace with his family.

In the Summer holidays our parents took us on outings and excursions by bus, mainly to the countryside. Even as young girls we could walk for miles on the moors, stopping for a picnic, and picking brambles or bilberries when the season was right. Dad would wander off saying he was looking for a sweetshop ... and much to our delight he always came back with lollipops (for years we thought there was a secret sweetshop inside Captain Cook's Monument!). He could be such fun. At the end of the day we pushed Mam up the hill to go for the bus home. Stewart Park, Great Ayton, Whitby and Scarborough were other places that we would travel to.

One adventure, though, was closer to home. A short bus journey found us at a place called Fairy Dell, near Marton. We walked beside the stream in the woods until, to our delight, we found a Tarzee. This was a rope, tied to the branch of a tree, with a short strong branch fastened to the other end of it that you could either stand, sit or hold on to. Taking turns, we swung to and fro over the stream clinging on to the short branch with both hands. We relished every moment laughing and giggling until Gilly for no reason suddenly let go of the rope! Landing hard on the dry ground, it looked as though she had broken her arm, but she was more bothered about her glasses. Dad knew from the cracking sound that he had to get her to the hospital. A family nearby gave Dad a towel to make a sling in which to support her arm. Scooping her up, Dad carried her to the nearest petrol station. Ann remembers a police car parked on the forecourt opposite Stewarts Park. The kind policeman had us all shoved up together in the back seat, taking care that we didn't knock Gilly's arm which was really hurting her. Putting on his sirens he quickly drove us home, before taking Dad and the little wounded soldier on to the General Hospital to have her arm set in plaster. We all agreed: what an adventure!

Life was changing at a fast pace and at the end of those Summer holidays we were due to start at the Senior School, St Thomas'. I always remember feeling really sick going back to school after the big holiday break. On our first day there poor Gilly was still wearing the plaster cast from her accident. The morning began with us anxiously waiting in the playground at school. The name of each pupil was shouted out, informing them of the class they would be in for that year. To our horror each one of us was in a different class. We had never been separated in school before and we all burst out crying. I felt that my right arm was going one way and my left arm another way! It was a long wait until break-time. Our first day ended with a girl called Jean, coming out of a PE lesson, being outraged because a teacher had shown her up in class. She began flicking her wet towel at any girl she passed. This included us as we started to walk home. Her intimidating behaviour continued until Gilly could stand it no longer. She pushed Jean to the floor and hit her on the head with her plaster cast! Someone grabbed my sister's hair to pull her off and I grabbed her hair in turn. Jean ran off and my younger sister gave chase. Thankfully Dad came round the corner and stopped the fight. Gilly had to go back to the hospital for a new pot because it had cracked in the fight. During our time at St Thomas' there was a lot of name calling aimed at us, especially from the boys: such as "matchstick legs, Snap, Crackle and Pop and anything else that had a three connotation to it. Consequently, we found it hard making new friends, with girls sometimes having difficulty in coping with the close and intimate relationship that we had as triplets. Often other families found it hard coping with three extra mouths to feed at teatime, but our friends were always welcome at our home.

Shortly after this I was to have my first period at eleven years of age. The facts of life were never talked about at home and it took the Lollipop Lady to gently explain to me that I wasn't going to bleed to death, but that it was just a normal part of growing up into a young woman. When I got home Mam took me upstairs, handed me a sanitary towel and belt and explained how to use them. Gilly started the day after me and Francy waited another year for her monthlies to arrive. Ann remembers Gilly taking her up to the bathroom and explaining "girly" things to her.

Our younger sister was left to fend for herself after we joined our new school. She had two years left in Sacred Heart School. From being top of her class Ann's schoolwork dropped due to her being bullied. She doesn't recall any help or adult intervention. Her next school was St George's Senior School. For the first time she no longer carried the label of being known as "the triplets' sister". All through her life Dad used to say, "We've got another one!" and she would be dragged from behind us when we were being fussed over by strangers.

The name calling and bullying stopped as we began to blossom into young ladies, with the boys taking a shine to us. They began following us around, always chasing us and wanting to play "tag". Dad often said, "Like bees around a honeypot". Near school was the training ground for Middlesbrough Football Club, on Hutton Road. A friend's house backed onto these fields and we would watch the young lads training, eventually becoming friends, but any new friendships were quickly nipped in the bud when Dad got wind of our connections with these football players!

CHAPTER 9 – FORGIVENESS

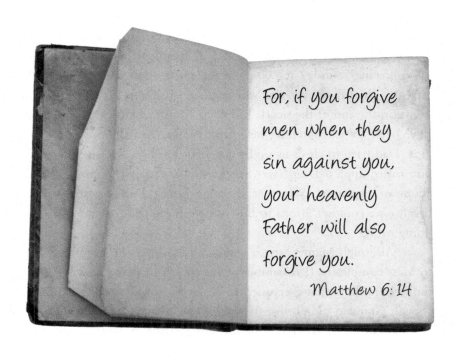

For, if you forgive men when they sin against you, your heavenly Father will also forgive you.

Matthew 6:14

At the end of 1968, just as we were settling into St Thomas' School, Grandad Leo (Mam's father) was told the heart-breaking news that he had cancer. It was a death sentence back then. I can recall our parents talking about Grandad's illness. Apparently, he had gone to hospital to have tests done to see how far the cancer had spread. Adults often speak as though children are not there and Mam came out with the sentence "He was riddled with cancer so they just stitched him up again". Another seed of fear was planted in me that day.

Uncle Alan would collect Mam each night to visit her father in North Ormesby Hospital. Early one morning Uncle Alan had some spare time so decided to pop in to see Leo. He found him sat up in the hospital bed enjoying a soft-boiled egg with "soldiers". Some of the yellow yoke fell onto his top, which upset him. Uncle Alan told him not to worry, as the nurse would change him later. It was 5th February 1969. He died that evening. A Requiem Mass was held on the following Saturday at 9.00 am. I remember Mam walking over the Green to the funeral car. She was wearing a black furry hat with pom poms on the end of the ties. It had been given as a gift from Grandma Lily. I felt so sad watching her. After the car had disappeared from view, Dad tried to cheer us up by taking us for a walk to the village to buy toffee apples. Death was another subject that was never talked about or explained. When Mam came home, Dad got shouted at because we couldn't afford to buy our treat! He couldn't do right for doing wrong.

Although Mam wasn't a regular church-goer she stopped going to Mass completely. (I remember crying myself to sleep every night for months thinking that everyone I loved in the family would die!) Even though Grandad didn't visit us very often, he must have dropped off our clothes and gifts. I have a memory of him walking out of the house and down the path with a soft and gentle look on his face. Unknown to the family, Grandad Leo had posted a letter to his sister, Win, on Tuesday 21st January 1969 (see appendix). He had written from his hospital bed on St. Vincent's Ward in North Ormesby, just 15 days before he died. He explained, "I am a little sore... managed to sit upright but how uncomfortable... fairly free of wind... saw the doctor and radiologist today and their only concern is the closing up of the hole in my tummy. At times I am inclined to be impatient... so many have gone out and are enjoying some freedom. Well, I mustn't let myself get too depressed... There is a slight improvement, however I have to stay put.

Mam's faith may have been shaken losing both her parents to cancer and very likely she was angry with God. I remember being out shopping with her and she would cross the road to avoid having to talk to people about her loss. Eventually she made an appointment to see the doctor. She was given small brown tablets to treat her illness. For a while I got a glimpse of a much happier mother as the tablets worked their magic. In hindsight she must have suffered most of her life with bouts of depression and Dad found that very hard to comprehend.

1955.

However, Mam had an artistic side to her personality. She loved painting, writing and crosswords. A drawing of Bambi , that she posted to her cousin in 1955, along with the painting of deer in the woods showcased her gifting, as does the following poem that came to light after her death:

You can't buy or borrow a minute,
Time's not for sale. Time is life
So waste not the runaway moments
in folly and worry and strife.
Time is a treasure more precious
than caskets of jewels ablaze.
So this is the wealth that I wish you;
good times, golden hours, happy days.

A new family moved into 15, Hereford Close on a warm sunny day, Mr and Mrs Greenheld and their five sons. Kath Greenheld soon became our Mam's new confidante and bosom pal. Our bedroom window was open and we watched the five young lads helping their parents to move all the furniture into the new house. We were shy but soon began laughing and waving each time one of them looked our way! New friendships began to bloom, with Mam often in the Greenhelds house having a cuppa and nattering with her new friend whilst their children all played outside in the fresh air. Gerard would often be part of our family either helping in the garden or out walking with us, for a romance was beginning to bud in his heart for one of us girls. Our Dad would be fully occupied fending off potential suitors in the years ahead, yet despite his best efforts we all had several love interests, leading to proposals of marriage.

My boyfriend, David, managed to pluck up the courage to ask my father for permission to marry me. He had proposed to me in the

Red Rose pub, where we did our courting. This was to Dad's delight, as they got on well together.

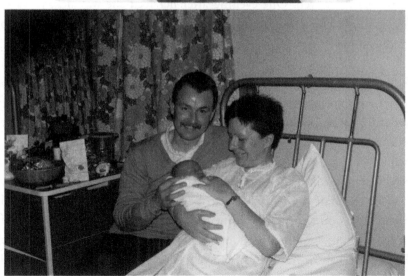

We married on the 9th August 1980, when I was twenty-three years of age. After five years of marriage I gave birth to our first child, James, by a caesarean section, as he was discovered to be laying in a breach position in the womb. Then four years later, pregnant with our second child, I was about to have a birth that would send me searching for my Heavenly Father.

After a trouble free pregnancy of nine months, I found myself exhausted during the throes of a twenty-hour labour. So a decision was made by the hospital staff to proceed with a ventouse or vacuum delivery. For this to go ahead the nurse put my feet up into stirrups in preparation; unfortunately one of the stirrups had not been fastened correctly to the post and my left leg fell to the bed. But two pushes later Jennifer was born weighing 9lb 1½ oz!

After her birth, I tried to stand, but my legs gave way and I collapsed. Later on, the specialist came to see me and just advised bed rest after my difficult labour. Because I had to stay in bed the nurses would pass my daughter to me for a feed and they would see to her other needs as well. One evening after her feed she was sick; it was a thick fluid, yellow in colour. The nurse said she would clean her up and told me to go back to sleep.

I was woken in the middle of the night to be told Jennifer had a blockage and needed an emergency operation to clear the obstruction. This couldn't be done in the James Cook hospital; so she would have to be taken to the Royal Victoria Infirmary in Newcastle which was nearly fifty miles away. I signed the consent forms and, when left alone, I cried and prayed to the God of my childhood, saying I was willing to suffer if He healed our baby. I was asked by one of the staff if I would like to be moved to a side ward and told them, "Do you want to finish me off altogether?!" I would have found it difficult to be alone with my anxious thoughts of our new baby undergoing an operation to remove a blockage. I felt so helpless and my vivid imagination had me picturing her being cut open from the top of her little chest to her tummy button! I was also comforted by the busyness of the maternity ward, where the other mothers pushed their cots to my bed for me to keep an eye on their babies whilst they showered.

The head midwife insisted that I should be x-rayed to determine why I was still having difficulty standing. It was discovered that I had suffered a separated symphysis (with my pelvic bones an inch apart) but what surprised the doctors was that most of my pain was at the base of my spine. My x-ray was put up near the nurses' station. I was told it was a common occurrence and was, therefore, surprised by the number of people who came to have a look at it.

The staff were very unhappy with me when I said that I wanted to travel by ambulance to Newcastle to see Jennifer. It was put to me that I might do more damage to my bones. After taking medication to help with the pain, I travelled to Newcastle by car with my husband, David, and our young son, as there were no ambulances available. At three years of age , James was a real handful in Intensive Care , dodging the wires of the intensive care incubators, but it was lovely to hug Jennifer and breastfeed her again. We managed another visit before Jennifer was returned to the ward in Carter Bequest five days later completely healed! I was told that sometimes blockages right themselves but I knew in my heart that her healing was due to God answering my cry. With the blockage gone, she began feeding as

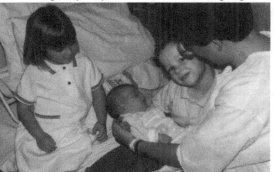

though she had never been away!

After a two-week stay in hospital I returned home. I was given a girdle to wear to help support my bones to heal, along with crutches to bear my weight. My bed had been placed in the dining room downstairs and a commode had been delivered, as I was unable to climb the stairs and placed in the front room, as we didn't have a downstairs toilet. David had taken six weeks off work to help care for his family but soon that was over and he had to go back. I began a long struggle with my health and was eventually told by the bone specialist that I needed an operation to pull my bones back together. This involved fastening a metal plate and screws to my pelvic bones, which is usually done for car crash victims. Although I was tired and depressed, I took the advice of my family doctor, which was to let nature take its course, as if I had the operation I would suffer with rheumatism in later years.

Immediately after Jennifer's birth, I put a complaint in to the hospital and over the following months attended meetings regarding my health and possible compensation, but this process was causing bitterness and unforgiveness in my heart.

A lovely friend called Olga had been collecting James to take him to and from school, but, as my ability to walk a bit further increased, I began to take him myself. I was in pain but it always eased when I sat down to rest my bones.

One rainy day, a new mum from school was talking to me whilst I was walking home and I invited her in for a drink, as it was raining, and we quickly became friends. Having previously spent time visiting various churches near home, I was searching for the God who had answered my prayer for Jennifer's healing. I realized that I had been unsuccessful in my quest, but after meeting my new friend Yvonne, I discovered she was a born-again Christian. I thought she had two heads but I recognized she had something "different" that I didn't have in my own life. She had peace and joy. Over the course of the next few months my life began to change for the better. I began to understand that Jesus loved me unconditionally, that he had died on the cross for me to set me free from my sins, that he wanted to have a personal relationship with me. I had my part to play in this divine exchange: to ask for forgiveness for my sins and wrongdoing to repent and invite Jesus Christ to be the Lord of my life, which is what I did. To my surprise and amazement I remember walking home that night after I made that decision, with a warm glow in my heart. I started to go to Coulby Newham Baptist Church and immediately felt at home. I would cry on and off for the next three years as the Holy Spirit began the process of healing my past, then one Sunday afternoon I returned home from Church and ripped up all the letters concerning my compensation claim. I had chosen to forgive the nurse for the part she had played in causing my ill health. Such joy and peace blossomed in my heart!

Even in my thirties it was important for me to share my new found faith with Mam and Dad, but as I did I couldn't understand their reaction. Dad thought I had become part of a cult and Mam didn't speak to me for three months. I gently tried to explain that God had put love in my heart for other people and that the Church only wanted to encourage me in my Christian life. It was at this time I saw a scripture in the Bible: Psalm 27 verse 10: "Though my father and mother forsake me; the Lord will receive me." This gave me comfort and I bought my parents a card each telling them how much I loved them.

Dear Dad

Did I ever say thanks
for all the toys you mended,
games we played,
outings to the park,
and the way you always
tried to cheer me
when I was down?
Did I ever say thanks
for the sacrifices you made
so I could be involved in
so many enriching activities:
Did I ever say thanks
for working so hard
to provide for our family?
Did I ever say thanks
for having such faith in me
and always being there
when I needed you.
Most of all did I ever say
thanks for caring?
DAD, I love you!

Dear Mum

Dear Mum
Did I ever say thanks
for all the meals cooked,
clothes mended,
stories told,
and the errands
you ran for me?
Did I ever say thanks for
being such a good listener
when I was down,
and making me feel like
I was the most important
person in the whole world?
Did I ever say thanks
for always being there
when I needed you and
for having such faith in me?
Most of all,
did I ever say
thanks for caring?
Mum, I love you.

Over the following year I kept pestering Francy to come to Church with me, saying it was so different to when we were children. Eventually she too accepted Jesus into her life! I was so happy but still in pain. Then one evening after returning home from a prayer meeting I could feel a circle of heat around my pelvic region! After a good night's sleep I opened my eyes and remembered what had happened the night before. Putting my feet gingerly to the floor I realized I felt different. Over the next few days my pain had nearly disappeared and I could walk much better. I recognized that God had healed me and was so grateful and thankful for being able to live life again! The following Sunday I told the Church that my bottom had been on fire! That caused a laugh. I have often wondered if my healing was linked to the forgiveness issue with the nurse?

Family and Church life continued over the years and I have never regretted my decision. Then in 2012 I found myself involved in a new church called Amazing Grace. This Church in Teesside has a vision for revival in Europe through preaching the Gospel. The New Testament teaching on grace is foundational and the heart of the Christian message. Several courses are run including Alpha, Route 61, A6 and M61. The aim is to have people healed of life's hurts, to be confident in the Gospel, to be filled with the Holy Spirit, to move in the freedom of God's power and to be secure in God's grace. I completed both the Route 61 course and the A61. The Route 61 course is a 12 week course based on a piece of scripture from Isaiah 6, a famous passage where Jesus describes what he came to earth to do. It is designed to help you experience Christianity. The A61 course is a 6 month training programme spread over a year based again on Isaiah 61. It is for everyone who is serious about going deeper with God.

It was after an A61 session on 'heart healing', that I was reminded of a scripture from Psalm 27:

Psalm 27
The Message (MSG)
A David Psalm

1   Light, space, zest—
      that's God!
So, with him on my side I'm fearless,
      afraid of no one and nothing.

2   When vandal hordes ride down
      ready to eat me alive,
Those bullies and toughs
      fall flat on their faces.

3   When besieged,
      I'm calm as a baby.
When all hell breaks loose,
      I'm collected and cool.

4   I'm asking God for one thing,
      only one thing:
To live with him in his house
      my whole life long.
I'll contemplate his beauty;
      I'll study at his feet.

5   That's the only quiet, secure place
      in a noisy world,
The perfect getaway,
      far from the buzz of traffic.

6   God holds me head and shoulders
        above all who try to pull me down.
      I'm headed for his place to offer anthems
        that will raise the roof!
      Already I'm singing God-songs;
        I'm making music to God.

7-9   Listen, God, I'm calling at the top of my lungs:
        "Be good to me! Answer me!"
      When my heart whispered, "Seek God,"
        my whole being replied,
      "I'm seeking him!"
        Don't hide from me now!

9-10   You've always been right there for me;
        don't turn your back on me now.
      Don't throw me out, don't abandon me;
        you've always kept the door open.
      My father and mother walked out and left me,
        but God took me in.

11-12 Point me down your highway, God;
        direct me along a well-lighted street;
        show my enemies whose side you're on.
      Don't throw me to the dogs,
        those liars who are out to get me,
        filling the air with their threats.

13-14 I'm sure now I'll see God's goodness
        in the exuberant earth.
      Stay with God!
        Take heart. Don't quit.

> I'll say it again:
> Stay with God.

I had been discussing my Catholic upbringing and had spoken about Middlesbrough Nazareth House with three other girls who had had very similar life experiences. The following day a booklet called Now & Then was dropped through my letterbox. The back page advertised a book entitled "The Memoirs of a Nazareth House Girl" by Anne Fothergill. My eyes nearly popped out of my head! What a co-incidence that this was the subject from the night before. I went straight to the Waterstones bookshop in the town and bought the last two books in the shop. I spent the rest of the afternoon immersed in the past and was overwhelmed to read on page 73 that "some late arrivals were admitted tonight, the Welfare brought them. Three little girls and they screamed the place down. Sister Joseph had them taken to the upstairs nursery." Could this be my sisters and I? The dates seemed to fit.

The following day I easily found Anne Fothergill's phone number in the directory and spent the next 45 minutes speaking to her. I was so excited and knew in my heart that the three little girls were us and Anne confirmed this the following day after asking her older sister about it.

In the following weeks I found myself remembering the unkind treatment, actions and works meted out by the Catholic nuns and priests: from being pulled out of assembly for not wearing the correct uniform right back to our parents leaving us in Middlesbrough Nazareth House in the first place. In my heart I felt God gently say, "As you forgive them, they too will receive forgiveness". I could feel tears springing to my eyes as I spoke out the names of the people that I chose to forgive and then the sun seemed to come out. It felt like a weight had been lifted off my shoulders. I realized that the Psalm also went right back to the night we were handed over, at four years of age, to strangers and that it was an antidote to some of the hurt and pain from my past experiences. As I continued to sit quietly reading this scripture the word "stronghold" stood out. I felt an impression of the Holy Spirit helping me to understand that God has a STRONG HOLD on our lives and that Middlesbrough Nazareth House was HIS BEST for us at that time and that it may even have been a place of safety. Suddenly I was no longer looking at these past experiences through the eyes of a child; I was now being shown the events through adult's eyes. I was learning to trust God with my pain and was slowly realizing that, like myself, many other men and women had been through painful experiences (some much worse than mine) that also needed God's healing touch.

Over the next few weeks a seed was sown of a Middlesbrough Nazareth House reunion taking place at Amazing Grace Church at Teesside Park. Plans began to take shape but I was so disappointed when nothing came of it.

As I shared my story with strangers outside of home I kept hearing the words, "You must write a book!" Over and over people kept giving me this instruction. Then one day after speaking to a family about Middlesbrough Nazareth House being on Park Road North, the husband said, "I lived on that road. You begin at the beginning and go from there". I knew then that I had run out of excuses! I also read a quote from Nancy Hoaz that stated:

There is a beginning, it's when I begin.
The middle is there as well ... the job
doesn't get done by itself. But once
we've done the best we can, the joy,
the sense of satisfaction ... and maybe
the buyers will come!

Chapter 10 – Fact or Fiction

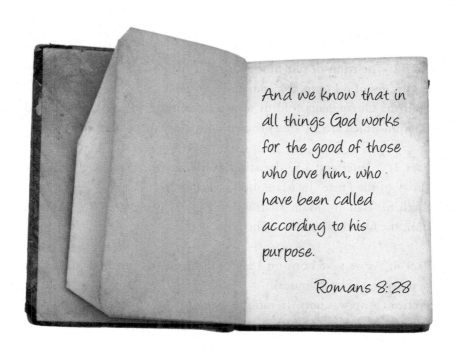

And we know that in all things God works for the good of those who love him, who have been called according to his purpose.

Romans 8:28

During the process of writing this book a treasure trove of hidden information has been uncovered helping us to have a greater understanding regarding our past family history.

Although we may have been dismayed by some of the decisions taken over fifty years ago by our parents, some crossed wires have been untangled enabling us to sort fact from fiction. In the 1960s it was possible to hear another conversation on your telephone line instead of the dialling tone. This situation too was called "crossed wires". Listed below are quite a few examples!

Fact 1: We were born full term at nine months weighing 5lb 9oz, 4lb 3oz and 4lb 3oz.
Fiction: We were always told we were born when Mam was only 7 months pregnant.

Fact 2: The truth of our time of birth is held on our individual birth certificates of 8.14 pm, 8.15 pm and 9.06 pm.
Fiction: Our parents told us we were born at 8.40 pm, 8.50 pm and 8.56 pm which are the times shown on the newspaper cutting.

Fact 3: A letter and a £3 donation would have been received from the "Privy of the Purse" by Mam, not a telegram.
Fiction: Told by Mam that a newspaper cutting and the telegram from the Queen were lost in the post.

Fact 4: As we were born on 18.5.57 and Ann was born on 31.3.59 we were separated by 22 months.
Fiction: Ann was born 18 months after us.

Fact 5: We had toys to play with as shown in our photographs.
Fiction: Told that as babies we had only each other to play with.

Fact 6: The truth is that our parents did a "moonlight flit" from Coventry as they were behind with the rent.

Fiction: We were under the impression that the family returned to Middlesbrough for Dad's employment.

Fact 7: Our parents brought the whole family to Middlesbrough believing 7 Windsor Road would be our new home.

Fiction: We always thought our parents hadn't made any provision for somewhere to live in Middlesbrough.

Fact 8: We were taken to Middlesbrough Nazareth House because Dad's pride got in the way of accepting financial help.

Fiction: We always thought the reason we were in Middlesbrough Nazareth House was down to Mam and, therefore, nothing to do with Dad.

Fact 9: The Welfare people placed us in the home.

Fiction: Mam said she took us.

Fact 10: We were in care from 15th July 1961 to 7th July 1962; a whole year!

Fiction: Told we were there for only 6 months.

Fact 11: Mam had poor health before she fell pregnant.

Fiction: I've always carried a burden believing Mam's ill-health as down to having us three!

Fact 12: Our parents had separated due to Dad's selfish, bad behaviour as well as his pride!

Fiction: Dad lived in rented rooms, as there was nowhere for him to stay in Grandad Leo's or Uncle Alan's house.

Fact 13: Several of the Nuns treated our family with kindness and compassion within the Catholic fold, providing us with clothing and support for Mam in her lack too!

Fiction: I always felt mistreated and unloved by the Nuns whilst I was growing up.

Fact 14: Dad and his brother, Ted, only ever freed one bear from a cage at the petrol station in Canada.

Fiction: Dad always told the tale of freeing hundreds of bears from traps in Canada. He was always good at story telling.

Fact 15: The Bible teaches that we are only to pray to God the Father, God the Son, Jesus, and God the Holy Spirit.

Fiction: As Catholics we were taught to pray to Our Lady and the Saints.

Whether our parents decided intentionally to withhold certain information concerning the earlier years of our upbringing or believed these facts ought to be concealed for our own good, we will never know. But as we have glimpsed into their trials and tribulations I personally have come to the conclusion that any past mistakes are to be forgiven.

Having the benefit of hindsight concerning past events, I am starting to understand that Dad provided love and comfort, as well as strict discipline. His gift to his daughters' was spending quality time with us as children and he was always happiest on our adventures around Albert Park and the Dorman Museum.

Mam's love language to us all was shown in her acts of service as she cared for us as children. Actions like cooking a meal, scrubbing the black mould off the walls in Mary Ann street, listening and supporting us with homework and issues from school as well as welcoming our friend into our home.

A photograph was received from Leeds Archives on 16.10.2014 showing the four of us standing in a garden with snow on the ground. After some quick research it came to light that Leeds Archive help deal with and support post adoptive services for families. This caused me to speculate that at the ages of five and three our upbringing may have been ' a different kettle of fish! '. (this is an English expression that may mean our circumstances would have become extremely unpleasant or trying). Although there is no evidence of any such action being taken, questions arise in me such as would we have been split up as sisters or even who would adopt or take on three little girls of the same age?

Although other children who passed through Middlesbrough Nazareth House may have travelled through distressing times, our saving grace is that we had each other, as triplet sisters.

During the research for my book the above subject seems to have come full circle. From the beginning of this journey I have experienced kindness and encouragement from total strangers, who have provided the insight needed to answer difficult questions that have risen along the way and in turn helped my sisters and me to become more comfortable with and accepting of our past.

As identical triplets we had a similar upbringing, but as individuals we have undergone a wide variety of experiences and emotions in our adult years. Personally one of my most important discoveries was that I have a heavenly Father who loves me unconditionally and desires to be involved in all aspects of my life, the good and the bad.

In chapter 9, I spoke about forgiving the nurse for the part that she played in my ill-health and in doing so joy and peace blossomed in my heart. Unforgiveness had been holding me captive to her and along with the struggles of everyday life I discovered I was depressed. This was a difficult period lasting several years, but let me encourage you to begin by forgiving small injustices. Ask Father God, Jesus or the Holy Spirit to help you in this task. Pray to be set free from bitterness, anger and hatred.

In the Bible there is a parable that explains how we become captives or prisoners. It is in the book of Matthew chapter 18 and it says the servant was unwilling to forgive and his master turned him over to the jailers to be tortured. It is imperative we forgive others to be set free ourselves. But some of you may say:

The person who hurt me will get away with it
The experience was too painful
I don't feel like it
It wasn't their fault
I can keep living this way

Another scripture in God's word, Galatians 6:7 states, ' Do not be deceived, God cannot be mocked. A man reaps what he sows'. Play your part, as I did, and TRUST God to judge fairly.

Maybe you have read my book and now realise you can have a personal relationship with Jesus because he loves you regardless of your past. If that is you and you would like to make a commitment, please pray the following prayer:

Lord Jesus Christ I am sorry for the things I have done wrong in my life and I ask your forgiveness. Thank you for dying on the cross for me to set me free from my sins. Please come into my life and fill me with your Holy Spirit and be with me forever. Thank you. Amen.

Rest assured that your life will be safe in His hands today, tomorrow and for Eternity.

So I began .... the middle is there as well.........the job didn't get done by itself.......but I have done the best I can.......there is a sense of satisfaction......even amazement that this book is nearly complete........I pray that the glory will go to the Holy Trinity .....oh the JOY.

Rosie Farrow.

APPENDIX – CHAPTER 3

Letters From Nazareth House
Sisters of Nazareth General Archive
Nazareth House, Hammersmith Road, London, W6 8DB
Telephone: 020 8600 6846

24/05/2013

Dear Mrs Sullivan,

Re: Rosemary, Frances & Gillian Farrow d.o.b. 18/05/1957

Thank you for your telephone call and subsequent letter enquiring about records for yourself and your sisters. Thank you also for enclosing stamps and a donation. I have passed your cheque to the Sister Treasurer and she has asked me to express her gratitude and has assured me that the money will be put to good use. It was lovely to see the "smiley" photograph of you and your sisters.

I have searched all the registers and record books for Middlesbrough Nazareth House and have found the following information. I'm afraid it does not really add to the details given to you by Sister Matthew.

In the <u>Middlesbrough Nazareth House Register of Children</u> I found entries for you at numbers 2780, 2781 & 2782. These entries recorded that you were born in Middlesbrough on 18/05/ 1957 and baptised at Saints Mary and Benedict, Coventry. I am enclosing your baptismal certificates. Your father was recorded as Frank Farrow, a "metal window fixer", and your mother as Irene Harcourt. It was noted that your parents were living and that your mother was a Catholic. You were referred to the Sisters by Father Dennett from the Middlesbrough Crusade of Rescue and you were admitted to Nazareth House on 15th July 1961. You left the home on 7th July 1962 when you returned to your parents.

I also found an entry in the Middlesbrough Nazareth House Address Book, which recorded your mother's address as 7 Windsor Road, Middlesbrough.

I'm sorry to say that these entries comprise all the information about you and your sisters in the archive. The Sisters did not keep case files at this time so the registers and record books are the only source of information about you. I'm very sorry not to be able to help you further as I realise you must have unanswered questions about this period of your lives.

Yours sincerely,

Christine Hughes
Archivist

CH: csn-Cl-321 1:24/05/2013

APPENDIX – CHAPTER 5

Sisters of Nazareth General Archive
Nazareth House, Hammersmith Road, London, W6 8DB
Telephone: 020 8600 6846

12/11/2014

Dear Mrs Gott,

Re: Middlesbrough Nazareth House July 1961-July 1962

Thank you for your telephone call regarding the time you spent with your sisters at Middlesbrough Nazareth House.

Firstly, you asked me whether child benefit continued to be paid to your parents while you were at Nazareth House or whether it was paid to the Sisters. As far as I know child benefit payments would have stopped during the period you were in care, and payments towards your maintenance at Nazareth House would have been made by the Crusade of Rescue or the Local Authority.

Secondly, you asked a more general question about what your life would have been like at Nazareth House. As you were only 4 years old when you were admitted to the home you and your sisters would have been placed in the nursery, where you would have been cared for by Sisters and perhaps lay staff or older girls from the Children's Home. Parents and friends were permitted to visit if they were able to. You would have been encouraged to learn about the Catholic religion and say simple prayers, but you would have had plenty of time for play and other appropriate learning too.

In the archive we have a contemporary account of life at Middlesbrough Nazareth House called <u>The History of the Foundation</u>. I have read this account for the year you lived at the house and have found the following information, which I hope you will find interesting:

July 1961	The children went to Redcar for 10 days summer holiday. They enjoyed lovely sunny weather.
Sep 1961	Work was commenced on a new nursery school.
Sep-Dec 1961	There were various visits from local dignitaries and charities. Visitors always brought presents for the children — sweets and fruit and clothing.
Xmas 1961	The children received many presents and were invited to parties, film shows, pantomimes etc. On the House Party night a film called "Come to the Stable" was shown.
7th Jan 1962	"The Friends of Nazareth House" provided an enjoyable concert, with the arrival of Santa Claus bringing suitable gifts to all.
March 1962	A group from Redcar gave an entertainment assisted by the Redcar Male Voice Choir.
5th April 1962	During the Home Office Inspection the Inspectors were very satisfied with the nurseries and children's rooms.
10th April 1962	Princess Margaret visited the town and the babies and children stood at the gateway to cheer as she passed, smiling to them all.
May 1962	25 girls had a week's holiday in Scarborough.
May 1962	The new nursery was working well. There were 23 babies aged 0-2 years and 29 babies aged 2-4 years.

June 1962   "The Friends of Nazareth House" held the annual trip for the children at Seaburn. The weather was good. The children saw the "Milk Tour of Britain Race" when the cyclists arrived at Seaburn. Denmark was leading by one and a half minutes, having beaten Britain who had been leading throughout the race.

I do hope the above information proves helpful.

Yours sincerely,

Christine Hughes
General Archivist

CH: csn-q-3653:14/11/2014

Sisters of Nazareth General Archive
Nazareth House, Hammersmith Road, London, W6 8DB
Telephone: 020 8600 6846

26/10/2015

Dear Mrs Gott,

Re: Middlesbrough Nazareth House

Thank you for your recent letter. I am glad the information I sent you in October has proved helpful.

In answer to your query about returning home to your parents when you were discharged from Nazareth House, I can only say that there was no strict protocol for this event. Often children were collected by their parents from Nazareth House. On other occasions someone from the Catholic Children's Society (Crusade of Rescue) may have taken children home. I have never come across a case where a Sister took children home.

I'm sorry that I cannot be more precise.
I do hope plans for the publication of your book are progressing well.

Yours sincerely,

Christine Hughes
General Archivist

CH: csn-q-3653:02/12/2015

APPENDIX – CHAPTER 9

Letter from St. Vincent's Ward, North Ormesby Hospital

St. Vincent's Ward
North Ormesby Hosp.
Middlesbrough
Teesside.
Tuesday 21st Jan

My Dear Den & Denny,

So sorry to have kept you so long without a letter, but a letter is a difficult operation. By now of course you will appreciate I am a little sore and it seems to come and go. However I've just managed to sit upright but how uncomfortable. At times I get bunged up with wind and with it an uncomfortable day. Today I am fairly free of wind. Saw the doctor and radiologist today and I think their only concern is the closing up of the hole in my tubing.

2

The other day I had a change of
catheter, this to try to check the
water flow – not really a flow but
enough to wet the bandage. I
thought I was drinking plenty of
water but the sister assures me
I'm not so now I have increased
to five or six jugs a day. I will
say that the urine is much clearer
and it has a lot of sediment to
get out of the bladder from the barb.
treatment. At times I am inclined to
be impatient and wonder if it is
all worth while and then bewan
the fact that so many have gone
out and enjoying some freedom. I
Well I mustn't let myself get too
depressed. I notice that Lily is
inclined that way and only last

night said "If only you were out it would save me visiting, I would be here earlier and it wouldn't matter if you couldn't do a thing." She is certainly regretting the shop now. The idea has been to get the mortgage wiped and then Lily could do as she pleased with it. In these days that isn't much. Even the papers are telling the people that the days of the corner shop are numbered. Well, we will just have to wait and see.

Today and yesterday there is signs of improvement and for about 36 hrs the dressing has not been wet. However I've still to stay put

and hope that it has stopped
finally. It is amazing how many
test have been taken. A thing
that has troubled me has been
a bowel convulsion which lasted
two to three minutes but now
that is better and lasts about half
minute.

Hope you are all keeping well
and enjoying the milder weather
also to hear of Bessie being so
improved

Will close for now with all
best wishes and love to all
from your loving
Lily + Leo

APPENDIX: THE KING & QUEEN'S BOUNTY

It was formerly customary for the Sovereign to dispense a bounty to parents on the birth of triplets. During Queen Victoria's reign a gift of £3 for triplets and £4 for quadruplets was presented to the family "when the children all survived: the parents being respectable but too poor to meet the unforeseen demands for providing for them at once". Applications were sent to the Keeper of the Privy Purse, who would reply asking for a letter testifying to the authenticity of the case from a doctor, clergyman or registrar of births and deaths. The donation would then be sent to the mother through the doctor, clergyman or registrar, who would sign and return a receipt for the money.

After 1938 the conditions were abolished and the bounty was thereafter recognised as being not so much a payment to help meet the extra expenses incurred, but as an honour which parents were privileged to receive from the Sovereign. In 1958, it was announced that the payment of bounty on the birth of triplets would cease and a message of congratulations would instead be sent by the Queen, in recognition of the occasion. This process continued until 1994.

ADDITIONS:

British Colonies.

British subjects who resided in the Colonies were also eligible for the Bounty, albeit through the recommendation of their respective Governor-General, who would forward the case to the Secretary of State for submission to the Sovereign.

Ireland.

In April 1923 the Irish Free State Government implemented a new policy with regards to the payment of the King's bounty to their citizens. They requested that all future applications regarding triplets born in the Irish Free State should not receive a 'Royal Bounty', but would instead be given a monetary contribution from the Irish Government, known as the 'State Bounty'.

ACKNOWLEDGEMENTS

This collective autobiography would not have been birthed without the support, additional memories and the love of my three lovely sisters, Ann, Gillian & Frances.

Thank you, Ann, for typing up this manuscript and for the laughs we have had along the way!

Cheers to Uncle Alan and cousin Anthony in providing snapshots of what life was like for our family during the 1950s & 1960s. Ant, you have kept me on my toes and encouraged me to continue to focus my attention and energy on the finer details of this book!

Heartfelt gratitude to my husband, David, for your patience support and excellent recollections of past history. In the Bible God says, "I will give you the treasures of darkness, riches stored in secret places so that you may know that I am the Lord, the God of Israel, who summons you by name" (Isaiah 45:3).

Robert Witts, you have been instrumental in accomplishing the task of unearthing the riches stored within the Coventry History Centre. Thank you.

Thanks also to Paul Stephenson for his help and kind permission to use his research contained in his book titled, Linthorpe and its village.

Thank you to Christine Hughes from the General Archive of the Sisters of Nazareth. My phone calls and letters have always been met by you having a pleasant, caring disposition, as well as the ability to shed light into my past.

Thanks also to Pam Clark from the Royal Archives for details of the King/Queens bounty.

I am very grateful for the resources I have used in my research from Middlesbrough Reference library, Teesside Archives and Dorman's Museum.

A big thank you to Jill Jackson, Izzy Russell and Vicky Prest. You each know the part you played.

Heartfelt gratitude toThe Christian publisher, Mark McKnight, who has helped my dream become a reality in print!

Many people have left their mark upon this book but hopefully the fingerprints of the Father, Son and Holy Spirit are all over it! I pray, Holy Trinity, that the account of my past blesses many people and gives you the glory you deserve.

Rosie Farrow
2016

SUICIDE

Help and support for anyone who is struggling with life can be obtained by contacting The Samaritans. Their website states:

Whatever you're going through, call us free any time, from any phone on 116 123.

We're here round the clock, 24 hours a day, 365 days a year. If you need a response immediately, it's best to call us on the phone. This number is FREE to call. You don't have to be suicidal to call us.

Lightning Source UK Ltd.
Milton Keynes UK
UKOW06f0109260117

292920UK00009B/43/P